THE EDUCATION OF
INNER MAN

*Essays on Religious and
Academic Idealism*

THE EDUCATION OF INNER MAN

Essays on Religious and
Academic Idealism

by

JOHN A. STOOPS

Dean, School of Education
Lehigh University

THE INTERSTATE
Printers & Publishers, Inc.

Danville, Illinois

Foreword

When *Religious Values in Education*[1] was published in 1967, many who were kind enough to read it thoughtfully were moved to ask me, "What is it that you believe?" The purpose of *Religious Values in Education* was to offer a view of man as *homo religiosus* and to study the problem of education from that perspective. I believe that when the public comes to accept that style of analysis, or one very like it, the question of religious education can be lifted from the establishmentarian and legal bog in which it now wallows. But until conversation on religious education reaches that higher ground of understanding, and until reforms are effected, public dismay over the work our educational institutions do in the value development of children and youth will continue. This is what I believe.

There are many more specific beliefs which I have come to hold regarding the educational development of the *inner man*. These are expressed in part by this series of essays which, in the main, constitute an exhortation for the humanization of the elementary and secondary school curriculum. The reader will recognize that the form of this appeal is discursive and is not based upon the contemporary modes of scientific inquiry. This implies no disrespect of the latter. But it reaffirms the fact that decisions about the education of our children are based primarily upon things which we value. *The Education of Inner Man* does not, therefore, attempt to meet the standards of educational science or analytical philosophy. Instead it is an intuitive approach to a number of educational concerns about which I think Americans feel strongly.

It is well to remember, however, that beliefs are organic. That is, they are never finished; they constantly grow. They are nourished at the root by constant experience and examination of ideas; their inclination upward is directed first one way, then another by elements in the environment in which they live, and they flower at various times in response to issues which arise. The beliefs expressed on these pages will continue to grow, and when seen at another time and place they may wear slightly different aspects. However, the inclination they show here has now achieved the stout stem of a hardy conviction.

---

[1] The Interstate Printers & Publishers, Inc., Danville, Ill.

Again, I wish to express appreciation to Mrs. John Stoops for technical assistance, to Mrs. Mary Barch for preparation of the manuscripts, and to Mrs. Faye Fenstermacher, Mrs. Catharine Boettger, and Mrs. Roberta Lareau for typing.

Table of Contents

Part I

THE DISORDERED WORLD
OF INNER MAN

Echoes of Dread

Order without, discord within
  The laws of sun and sky
Cosmos about, chaos within
  In order do imply
Method abounds, muddle within
  Serenity is nigh.
Power surrounds, weakness within
  But man is moved to sigh,
Nature exalts, despair within
  His inner world's awry,
Learning defaults, anquish within
  Torn with the question "why,"
Life goes on, dread within
  And knowing he must die.

Prefatory Remarks:
The Philosophy of Dread

In general, Heidegger is credited with the most direct and forceful formulation of the notion of dread. Each human, at some early stage of awareness, becomes conscious that his earthly life is an interval. He does not know *why* he exists; he knows only *that* he exists. He does not know *why* this life ends; he only knows *that* it ends. Dread, or *Angst*, is recognition of this basic human predicament. It is a sensing that existence emerges from nothingness and when its interval ends resolves into nothingness. Existence, therefore, is the interval between nothingness and nothingness, and the awareness of this is dread.

One need not delve into the theoretical problems of nothingness to appreciate the problem of dread. One need only understand that dread forces each individual into a quest for a meaning-of-life. If existence is an interval, then the task falls to each existing individual to overcome the absurdity of a meaningless existence. Dread forces the inner world of man into a condition of disorder. In order to fulfill the basic condition for happiness, one must come to terms with dread. This is done by creating an inner order which gives meaning to existence. Needless to say, any form of education which does not help the individual find meaning is inadequate.

Religious education deals with this matter. Used in this sense, the term religious education denotes a much larger activity than schooling on establishmentarian ideas and dogmas. However, most modern religious establishments do teach religions which provide help for the individual who accepts these teachings. But, increasingly, less and less of organized American education is conducted within religious establishments. One possible result of this is that the inner worlds of men are shut off from this source of inner order. There is much in modern life to suggest that the disorder of inner man is greater than before.

The three essays in Part I—Work, Love, and Ordeal of Ideals—are concerned with symptoms of the disorder of inner man. They are efforts by the writer to depict the turmoil and discontent of a people who have more of the external reasons for happiness than any who have preceded them

3

in time, but who seem to have little power to command the internal forces which must be aligned for a meaningful existence. Although the philosophy of dread appears a pessimistic aspect of the philosophy of being, it does show that human happiness is possible for those who take charge of their own existence and move with courage in a world of choice.

WORK

HOW'S IT HOLDING? Many professors are compulsive talkers. Any incident, however mere, can be elevated to endless monologue by a university prolocutor in top form. This capacity is epitomized in certain academic men who really say nothing, but who never fail to make a point of saying it both constantly and well. Seldom can such men be inspired to the heights of silence.

And a good thing it is, too; many a professor makes an otherwise dull course sufferable by deliverance of graceful and propitious lectures. But we cannot expect these elegant utterances simply to cease when the professor departs his classroom and moves about in a world of ordinary events. Accordingly, the public press is constant witness to and the public forbearance is constantly tested by seemingly learned exhortations and declamations which come in never ending flow from American centers of higher learning. Silence can be beautiful, but professors, alas, are seldom silent.

When it happens, the occasion is worth noting. A few years ago, one such professor, well known for his volubility, lived in an ancient house with an enormous slate roof, which, by responding to the inevitabilities of time and nature, had fallen in to a condition of disrepair. The roof was leaking, and bits of lifeless slate were falling off with increasing incidence. As might be expected there was much fulmination about this, some of it in professorial style, but much of it in words which seldom appear in pedagogical discourse. Despite this, the ruin continued to spread and it soon became obvious that someone was needed who could do more than *talk* about roofs.

Appeals for help went out in the usual form, but workmen who install and repair slate roofs, even then, were precious. At last one was found. The professor, a model of lucidity, telephoned his need. The roofer, using a Dutch vernacular, agreed to a visit with an economy of words which the professor found nothing less than frightening. But, soon other weeks had gone by, the promised visit did not occur, and the professor again began to worry. The roof continued its flaking and falling, but another call was contemplated with disrelish. Even windbags are reluctant to make phone conversations characterized by long and unremitting periods of silence at the other end.

But one day as the professor was out tending his yard he sensed another presence. Turning, he found a greying, blue-dungareed man of middle sixties some distance away, gazing intently at the roof. He promptly went over to open a conversation, but he was ignored. His intolerance of taciturnity urged him into several other false starts. These met with equal indifference from this laconic companion. At last, then, with a mighty shrug, the professor fell into verbal repose, and the two men stood together and stared at the roof, one stanchly mute and the other mildly befuddled.

A silent quarter of an hour thus passed, but at last the roofer turned and in two words suggested a cost for the project. It was far below what the professor had expected. He quickly assented, but as he continued to discourse on his satisfaction, the roofer turned on his heel, walked to his car, got in and drove away.

Months passed and nothing happened. The professor began to fear there was a misunderstanding, but upon reflection he found it difficult to see how this was possible. One day, in late fall, a truck arrived with a stack of fresh new slate. However, a pile of slate is not a roof, and soon the wind began to howl derisively through and across the random openings above. This weird housetop fanfare celebrated the arrival of every breeze that blew throughout the long winter. The occupants noted the changes in timbre, note, and key, as the holes became larger and changed in shape. But spring did come and the pile of snow melted from atop the slate in the yard. It was no longer new, no longer fresh, but a new season of Hope had arrived.

One morning at daybreak the household was aroused by the sound of scratching and hammering above. The professor stepped outside and saw his friend scurrying across the surface of the roof, using his hands with a skill and efficiency which no one could fail to admire. Decayed slate was literally flying in all directions. But the roofer ignored his audience which soon stopped its gazing and departed. That evening, upon his return, the professor was astounded and enthralled to find a beautiful new roof in place and the anticipated traces of the old one nowhere to be found. The quality of the work elicited the wonder and awe of the entire neighborhood. The professor expanded on this. He talked on and on about certain kinds of things being worth waiting for.

Months passed, and at last the expected bill came. It was 40 dollars under the estimate! By this, the professor was nearly stunned to silence, but not quite. First, being certain there was no mistake, he began to discuss the whole matter as an agreeable experience in cultural interaction. To his friends he suggested that one does not need to travel to the other side of the world to find men who are unusual, etc. Integrity is not dead. To his students he declared that the uneducated of America have great gifts to offer if we can pause from our studies long enough to consider them.

Then seasons came and passed, and his interests moved to other subjects. After a year the matter was well-nigh forgotten. But, late on a summer afternoon of the following summer, the professor was tending his yard and he sensed the presence of another. Turning, he found a greying, blue-dungareed man in his middle sixties gazing at the roof. The professor joined him, and as was by now their custom, the two men looked upward in silence. After a time the roofer turned to the professor and said, "How's it holding?" The professor replied, "Fine." The roofer looked up again; there was a trace of a smile on his face. Nothing more was said. The roofer walked to his car, turned, looked upward; again there was a trace of a smile. Then he seated himself, closed the door, and drove off. This time the professor was silent and he remained silent. He had much to think about, and it was some time before he had anything to say.

THE EDUCATED MAN. This was one of those all too rare moments which brings a professor (or anyone else) to ponder: What is an educated man? Our scale of academic values and degrees suggests one kind of answer, but it is not an answer which satisfies every condition. Our civilization declares that the professor is educated; certainly he is more educated than the roofer. But is he? The professor serves with his words but the roofer serves with his tools. One articulates ideals in sentences and paragraphs, but does not the other articulate ideals as well?

In the roofer's fleeting glance at this newly made roof the professor saw that which gave him to pause. The professor, of course, owns the house. A deed is recorded which attests to this. The roof is on the house. There is no question in the law who owns the roof. But who *really* owns that roof? A man put something of himself into it. When this same man passes by and looks at the house he sees something of himself there. Here is a roofer who seldom speaks, but he can drive about a community looking at rooftops and seeing something of his life and the incarnation of his ideals in the skyline of his town. Why else would he worry (after he was paid) whether or not the job held well. No, there was more to this than a man making money. This, it seems was an example of a man being a man.

In that same sense, can anyone ever own a Rembrandt? Can anyone ever possess a work by Shakespeare? When it comes to buying and owning, one can be said to be legally in possession of a Rembrandt or of an early folio of Shakespeare's work. But in the full course of things, the work of these artists forever bears their names. Finlandia is a musical poem dedicated to a country and a people, but it belongs forever to Sibelius. He could not give it away because he is in it. He goes wherever it goes. When the music sounds, Sibelius is heard. As the orchestra plays, Sibelius lives. We say that in this way the painter, the author, the composer is immortal, and so he is.

Why not also a workman? Those high on a scaffold repairing the stonework of a renaissance cathedral are in a strange and somewhat obsequious communication with those prideful masons of yore whose flesh and bones are now dust but whose work is proffered before them in strength and splendor. It is there in the rugged eloquence of cleanly dressed stones. The mason's pride, his integrity, his ideals—all are there. And as the trowels of today dig into the loose and crumbling mortar, the marks of erstwhile workmen are exposed. See how they did this? What a remarkable cut! How did they ever get such a large stone this high? Who put this one in its place? A journeyman? Or was it a young apprentice fitting his first under the critical eye of the master mason? Did a man, long ago, end his day, or perhaps his life, with the placement of that stone? These stones wear the ideals of men, and all of us are joined by them, not only to the builders of renaissance cathedrals, but also to the first man who worked upon a stone and, thereby, began man's long adventure of imposing will and idea upon the materials of the earth.

In the work men do lies immortality. It is there or nowhere. In their work also lies their mortality, their life. A man is not being selfless by doing his work well. As he approaches the central tasks of his life he is establishing his selfhood. One who has not, in the course of his development, established some mode of service which he does well, which establishes him as a being of worth, remains an unknown, a possibility, and nothing more. Whatever else he can do or say, we cannot concede that he is educated.

Who is better educated, the professor or the roofer? One serves by putting ideals into language, the other serves by putting ideals into buildings. The issue is not resolved on the grounds of academic degrees and scholastic laurels. How well does each man live his life? A large portion of a man's life is his work. There can be good roofers and good professors. We cannot say that one is better educated than the other.

There is more which can be learned from the relationship of the two. The roofer in his work was not in the "hire" of the professor any more than the professor who teaches the roofer's son is in the hire of the roofer. The roofer was not "selling" his labor. He did not ask the professor if the professor "liked" the roof. He asked only, and for his own information, if the roof leaked. Likewise, the professor would not ask the roofer if he "liked" the way his son was taught. Such questions as he might ask would be for *his* own information. It is important to understand what this means.

What governs such men? Clearly they are responding to ideals which are within them and are sovereign to them. To such men these ideals are autonomous and not subject to melioration. Roofers and professors, lawyers and carpenters, masons and physicians—all are distinguishable by the ideals of the work to which they are devoted. In each case the ideal is sovereign to economic considerations, sovereign to friendship, and sovereign even to service. Men are both freed and enslaved by the ideal.

One does not tell a man of this kind how to do his work. Payment for the job does not purchase the right to intrude upon the divine relationship between craftsman and his ideals. Such intercessions diminish a workman's sense of worth. One may employ a surgeon to perform a needed operation, but despite the importance to all concerned the patient or his next of kin may not direct the surgeon's performance of his duties. After the surgery the surgeon may visit the patient and ask questions. Like the roofer, he wants to know, "How is it holding?" He, too, in his work, was responding to an autonomous ideal. His judgment of himself is far more severe than that invoked by the patient.

However, we do have professors, carpenters, and surgeons who are not governed by ideals. Their work satisfies at times and at other times it does not satisfy. This is because their concern does not outdistance the customer's concern. Slogans such as "The customer is always right" or "We aim to please" offer the suggestion that the worker plans to be patronizing. In any case, it does not reflect an appropriate attitude. It does not suggest that the worker derives integrity from an ideal. He can, of course, be an honest man, but he is simply selling his time to another in need of his services. The employer during this time is his "boss," and he accepts this relationship in consideration of the sum paid him. This is slavery by consent, but it is nonetheless slavery.

Behind every task which is to be done is a perfect conception of its performance.[1] When a worker is commissioned for a work, those who select him pay for his reputed conception of the performance of the task as well as for his reputed ability to fulfill that conception. He need not ask, "How do you want me to do this?" "Would you rather I do this first or that first?" An authentic craftsman, if he asks such questions, does so out of a compulsion for congeniality and not out of a need of direction or assurance. If he is committed to the ideals of his craft he will set about to incarnate these ideals in his creations. Once underway on a task, nothing else that he hears matters.

All of these things combine to suggest there is a philosophy of work which is an aspect of the philosophy of man. Americans need to pay attention to the philosophy of work which seems to be growing and taking effect in the present century. There are clear indications that it is changing from what it was to something new. Moreover, the changes evident suggest that the emerging philosophy of work takes something away from men and the quality of their lives. It is a loss which should be examined philosophically. We can't in these times make the claim that men are better educated if the effect of our schooling is to devalue something which is so prominent an aspect of their being, as is work. A manual workman alive to the ideals of his work is, therefore, better educated than a man plied with academic credits but who does not contain within him a summons to a standard of performance which is autonomous or sovereign to all else.

THE DEVALUATION OF WORK. "Work" is a homely little Anglo-

---

[1] Richard M. Weaver, *Ideas Have Consequences* (Chicago: University of Chicago Press, Phoenix Edition, 1948), p. 73.

Saxon word. As words go it is not pretty or pretentious, but it represents that activity which stands near the very center of a man's existence. Probably no choice a young person makes is of greater critical importance than his choice of work. Probably nothing among his predispositions matters so greatly as the attitude he brings to that which he will call his work. Few things can matter more in determining the quality of his life than the ideals which govern the quality of his work.

What is it that a man means when he says, "I must find work"? To most Americans now this simply refers to an occupation which will furnish an income which makes other things possible, such as support of a family and provision for other experiences which yield pleasure. Work in this sense is something that is done in order to achieve other things which come as a consequence of the work's having been done. Therefore, one is sustained in the "work" that he does by the thoughts of the rewards which come afterward. In the parlance of modern social discourse, we speak of this kind of "work" as a job or as employment. Social theories want all men to have jobs. However, those subtle traditions which only the discerning sense in our language suggest the word "work" is something different than "job" because "work" is something more.

We do not have at our disposal a reliable history of the attitudes which have been borne in the course of our civilization toward this thing called work. However, there is good reason to suppose that the attitudes which have developed in America over the past years differ in some respects from those of earlier times. There is also good reason to suppose that implicit in the modern attitude there is a pervasive devaluation of work. The consequence of this is that a vast number of our citizens spend roughly a third of their lives involved in activities which they dislike and from which they derive little in the way of personal satisfaction.

The history, if it could be written, would probably show that work and the working man and his ideals were abused by those who rose to great wealth mainly upon the work that others did. It would show also the advent of machines, automatic devices, which have provided many jobs composed of routine and repetitive activity. Human work which requires sheer physical effort has almost vanished, and the future promises that even complex intellectual procedures will be more and more performed by computers. Human work, therefore, will move even further in the direction of evaluation, judgment, planning, and communication. Now even routine and repetitive types of work are disappearing.

It is against this background we see the pervasive devaluation of work, as those who lead the front of American labor continue their preoccupation with the benefits which are external to the work itself, which come only as a consequence of its being finished, and which bear only a very remote relationship to the work itself. This is not a suggestion that the worker is not entitled to the full fruits of his work. He should be and must be. But those whose work it is to guard the interests of workmen need to look more broadly at the human need to work, to learn if there are not other kinds of benefits which have not been discussed in bargaining.

The history of this problem might show that 100 years ago American farmers had achieved a degree of personal independence greater than anything known by a significant group of people. The farmer and his family operated their own enterprise. They were sustained by it, and they gained spiritual strength from it. In the brief course of the last 50 years this bastion of independence has all but crumbled. Now the American agricultural system is sustained by a vast system of bounties which are given to farmers for not planting crops, not raising livestock, and not doing the things which by training they can do and which, by their nature, they want to do. In recent years legislators and other government officials have been heard to denounce some of our rural citizens for making use of land they were being paid not to use.

Of course, it will be shown that economic conditions made necessary farm subsidies and price supports, but what has come to us in one time of our history as a temporary solution to a crisis appears now to stand as a permanent national policy. A whole generation of Americans has grown up under this scheme, and all of the relevant moral issues are there. Again, it is a devaluation of work and the absence of good, honest thought on the policy which has robbed the American farmer of much of his dignity and most of his independence.

Another indication of the devaluation is the omnipresence of gambling in its most outright form. It goes on in many ways: perhaps its most sophisticated form is in speculation in stocks and real estate. Everywhere men build castles in air, and they yearn for happy accidents. There is an American reverie—what is the American dream? It is to accumulate a fortune simply by paper, stock, real estate or grain transactions and no real work.[2] Authorities on the stock market will soon inform a speculator what a barren, sterile, and forlorn thing his dream is, but it goes on. Other consequences of the devaluation of work can be easily seen. One is the flight from boredom, a flight which leads one to experience trauma, sex, drugs, or violence, and often ends in debauchery or degradation. There is in this loss of capacity for keen enjoyment, a loss of a sense of purpose. Gone are the exciting goals, the dreams of achievement, and the aspirations of a kind which keep men alive and moving.

Although we can assert the American labor movement has a just purpose and an honorable history, and that those associated with it today are among the finest men to be found anywhere, it is also true that all the history has not been honorable, all of the men have not been just. More than a few became corrupt traders in the work of other men. Certainly these have been attracted to the labor movement because the power of the united workmen also holds the promise of getting more by giving less. When men unite around such a theme they can be assured that those who live and dream by such codes will be attracted to them, will stand with them, and ultimately will come to lead them. America has now and has had in the past great labor leaders. But greedy job holders make it difficult for a great leader to serve.

Thus, in many cases the laboring man no longer stands with dignity but with arrogance. His work is not part of him. It is something external to him, and his real involvement is a feverish striving for money, benefits. At the same time, he deprives himself of the natural pleasures of his job because the whole motive for work is not giving but getting, not making but acquiring, not serving, but being served, not creating, but bargaining with moments, hours, and weeks of life in exchange for forms of wealth which are needed at other times and places. His progress is measured by inches gained in the tug of war with those who employ him.

This history could become a veritable polemic against the style of life chosen by modern America. Many circumstances of American life which could be brought forward display the irony that the most industrious and materially prosperous people in the world are in a constant wrangle over ways to do less work and achieve greater

---

[2] Phillip H. Phenix, *Education and the Common Good* (New York: Harper and Brothers, 1961), p. 99.

rewards. Everyone seems involved. Teachers, physicians, farmers, laborers. Veritably no group has not been heard from. All, of course, is not lost. In recent years the labor unions have been developing a class of reflective men who see their mission more broadly. Those whose thoughts are respected in American life are turning to this problem. The full light of hope will beam when America's vast educational enterprise turns to the task.

THE ILLUSION OF LEISURE. It seems probable that the propensity of man to class himself in a hierarchy is the principal cause of the derogation of work. The illusion persists that somehow the class above, be it middle, upper-middle, or higher, has less work and more leisure. Therefore, a man is not unreasonable if he believes that a life of less work is a symptom of his own human advancement and a testimony to his personal success. The struggle between class groups has this or something like this at its center. If a man can increase his share of the abundance of the world while at the same time having more time to do nothing at all, he is making progress upward. After all, the illusion shows, the upper classes have complete abundance and complete leisure.

Enough of this is true to give the illusion solidity. A worker trudges to his home on a winter evening. The society section of his newspaper sports photographs of well-to-do citizens sprawled on resort beaches or wading through snowdrifts aboard skis. The airline ads in television show entrancing scenes in far-off parts of the world with beautiful people in colorful settings with exotic foods and drinks. There is the light-hearted suggestion of fun, excitement, and romance. The heft of a golf club, the wallop of a tennis ball, the feel of a casting rod, the pull of a sailboat are surely the essence of the good life. Even Aristotle asserted that the end of work is leisure.[3] So there is solidity in the illusion. Isn't it nice to go into a hotel and not have to carry your own bag? Sometimes the company offers a bonus, a surprise. It will arrange for junior executives to confer with each other for a week in one or another of the plush places of the world. So they roam about a highly reputed "bower of bliss," and in unoccupied moments they tell each other how great it is. The more discerning, however, begin to note that after the fourth day

---

[3] *Nicomachean Ethics*, Book Ten, Chapter Nine, "Again happiness seemingly requires leisure; for the object of our labor is to gain leisure, as the object of war is to enjoy peace."

it gets a bit thin. But even these refuse to admit it aloud because confession that one has trouble with an excess of leisure and luxury is tantamount to admitting that one really belongs to a lower class.

Let us suppose there is a group called upper class. Who belongs to it is anyone's claim or guess. Probably anyone's list would include those who have great material wealth. Like any group there are those in it who are wastrels and really do very little of anything for very long. Are there any more of these among the wealthy than any other group? It is to be doubted. Those who are in a class called wealthy, if anything, work harder than do those in the classes which are less wealthy. A study of the activities of wealthy families soon shatters the illusion of unremitting leisure. While they do turn up at resorts and make globe-encircling trips, they work. They are busy, active, driving humans fascinated by enterprises of all kinds. If there is a superior value in the life of the well-to-do, it is in the variety and intensity of their work interests. Therefore, if one wishes to emulate the class which he fancies to be above him, he will throw himself into a variety of things, not buy his wife a mink stole and send her on a tour of museums. The wealthy do not tour museums, they pay for them and work in them. This is how they make their lives something of worth.

Yet the illusion persists. Recent publicity has been given to the notion that the miracle of American technology is about to create a life of leisure. In the wake of this a number of writers have suggested that *education for leisure* is a thing to be developed by the schools. Some essays have envisioned an outright fun and games curriculum. One such writer in preparing an article made a list of men in his community whom he considered well educated. His purpose was to ask each of them for an opinion on what *education for leisure* might be. His first trouble occurred when he discovered that his well educated men were so busy it was difficult to arrange an interview. His second trouble was that the well educated men had so little leisure that they had little or no idea of what to do with leisure. They generally anticipated no such time, and if such time did come they would use it for the pursuit of work ideas which had been too low in priority to win a place in their crowded schedule.

If neither the wealthy class nor the educated class is preoccupied with leisure, then what is the problem? The problem is in the illusion that leisure is an uncontaminated good. A very well known public school superintendent joined a university faculty with a hard-won feeling of relief. He thought professors were a leisure class. Some professors are leisure-borne, but this erstwhile superintendent soon, to his surprise, found himself working as hard as ever. Speaking to his former colleagues, he said, "Don't you believe that university life is easy." What really happened was the superintendent, a well educated man, found in the university environment a vast number of new interests which evoked strong responses from his intellectually vigorous nature. He would be the same anywhere.

Education must destroy the illusions that achievement is apart from work, illusions that movie stars do little but sit around trying to decide what pictures to be in, illusions that sports stars do little but wait for the events, and illusions that business men spend most of their time at golf. The greatest, and in the end, the most cruel illusion of them all is that leisure is an unmitigated good. No one who is retired but able to work feels rewarded by being told that he is expected to do nothing.

THE AUTONOMOUS IDEAL. Education must restore the autonomous ideals of work which were perpetuated so beautifully by the apprentice system that dominated trade education over the centuries and that was dominant also in the guild relationships of medieval universities. Craftsmanship and scholarship both contain ideals which are autonomous.[4] The craftsman has in his mind a perfect conception of rendering the task; the scholar has in his mind a conception of a truth, which exists for its own sake, without extraneous end, aim, or purpose. Both of these archetypal visions can inspire great work. No one is educated for leisure; the notion is anathema. If one is educated for a life of meaning, he is educated for commitment; he is educated for work. Yes, the task is more difficult because many modes of American industry do not give a worker a complete work to do. Many workmen have only routine and repetitive aspects of a work in which many participate. Still, a workman can be made to see and feel that it is his work. He can establish a standard or an ideal, and he can draw joy in its accomplishment. It is easier to do this when his effort includes planning, rendering, and evaluating the complete task, but it is surely not impossible to organize assembly line duties so that the workman can sense his accomplishments.

---

4 Richard M. Weaver, *op. cit.*, p. 76.

Certainly a first step in the re-appreciation of work is advocacy of the autonomous ideals of work. In *industrial arts* and in *home arts* educators can teach that in each work that stands to be done there is an ideal through which the worker can find his own integrity and worth. Taken in this light, a "shop course" is not simply an exercise in technology. It is a form of humane teaching which opens a way for a boy to become something more of a man than he would otherwise have been. Industrial arts education, at its best, is one of the humanities. If it is not one of the humanities, it should be dropped from the curriculum. The apprentice master not only gave a boy skills; he gave him ideals, and through these ideals he gave him self-worth, and through self-worth dignity, and in the end he gave him a personal meaning. All of these things add up to a liberal education and a free man. Whether he could read or write well was only incidental. Industrial arts does not give a boy a trade, but it can help him with all the rest.

A second step is to destroy the illusion that human advancement is accomplished by attaining leisure. Man in poverty spends more meaningless, directionless hours than man in affluence. Men who openly seek leisure are on the way down, not up, the scale by which modern men value and class themselves. Schools and churches need to make more of this point. The saying which goes, "If you want a job done seek a busy man" is a great deal more than "homespun" philosophy. Again, it is an avowal of the philosophy which moves toward first principles. Men in their happiest state are in some form of meaningful enterprise. Therefore, social action which *creates* and *gives* to men income-producing "jobs" cannot be an adequate formula for a good life. There must be also an environment of autonomous ideals in which a man finds and knows his work.

Probably nothing can dispel the tinsel illusions and jerry-built expectations of leisure more quickly than the study of biographies of men who achieved recognized greatness in western civilization. When one participates in the life of a great man through the offices of a sensitive and skillful biographer, he is brought to sense the things which inspired greatness in the subject. Thus, in the presence of greatness, the reader finds that money, if money there was, was incidental, and if it turns out there was much money, the money often became a nuisance, a source of unhappiness and misunderstanding. No, great men achieved greatness in their work and in their work alone; and in the end, the work of a great man became the man himself. We forget his size, his shape, his property, even his manners. In the end we reflect mostly upon the great work which became his life.

Education in school and church must, therefore, go far beyond a concern for skills in contemplating what must be done to get children and youth ready for the work of their lives. We are very close to accepting money and social prestige as the autonomous ideals for work. Even though nearly every thoughtful man recognizes this posture as hollow and ultimately unrewarding, we go on counseling and writing to young people that education means a better job and better prospects for enjoyment. We are deceiving them when we suggest that a better job is one which pays more and that better prospects for enjoyment mean more leisure. We ought to be giving them things in which to believe. The strange and wonderful thing about all times is that young people know this, and in their own way they attempt to defeat the cynicism of the institutions which teach them. There is a perennial majesty in the truth of the young.

LOVE

Love is money; money is love. No idea in American life has been more traduced and derogated than the idea of love. This is a great loss, and the lives of Americans are diminished because of it. We are accustomed to think that only those who live in ghettos, feeling pangs of creature hunger, are deprived. But even the affluent are deprived when a great and ennobling possibility of existence has been taken from them, and this, it seems, has happened. The idea of love has been removed from the realms of mind and vulgarized on the counters where obscenity, cosmetics, and voluptuousness are turned to profit. The idea of love has been removed from the realms of mind and transformed to a neurosis in the counseling chambers where the various hacks of psychoanalysis make their fortunes. The world has turned on friends and lovers. They have become means rather than ends. Those who feel love must guard or conceal this feeling from the many among us who would convert it to a selfish advantage. A lover is fair game in an acquisitive culture. He is not respected.

In such circumstances it is appropriate that we turn to another time, another civilization, another frame of reference. Perhaps, in classical antiquity, men were not so disposed as we to impoverish their lives and diminish their being; and in regard to the nature of love itself, it is appropriate that we turn to Plato's *Symposium*[1] which holds distinction as a great work of literature and a work of philosophy. There is no question that it is the most complete statement on the nature of love which we have from Plato. It is a great work by a great man. It was written during the prime of his philosophic life. Never has there been a more appropriate tribute to an author than the suggestion by Alfred North Whitehead that "the safest general characterization of the European philosophical tradition is that it consists of a series of footnotes to Plato."[2] The *Symposium* is but one of

---

[1] All quotes in text, except where otherwise indicated, are from B. Jowett, *The Dialogues of Plato* (New York: Random House, Inc., 1937), pp. 301-305.

[2] Alfred N. Whitehead, *Process and Reality, An Essay in Cosmology* (New York: The Macmillan Company, 1929), p. 53.

his works, but it can furnish the food for many long winters of thought.

APOLLODORUS. The book opens with three men in a friendly conversation which results in two of the three, Glaucon and his companion, appealing to the third, Apollodorus, to recount the speeches about love which were held at a banquet in the home of Agathon, an Athenian poet many years ago. Apollodorus, who for the past three years had been studying with Socrates, was just then in the flush of discovering himself as a philosopher and considered himself "not ill-prepared" to comply. First, he reminds his listeners that the event took place many years ago, while he (Apollodorus) was still a boy. His knowledge of the speeches came from Aristodemus, who was there, and, as a devoted student of Socrates, remembered the speeches in detail. Plato, by having men repeat speeches which had been given at an event which could have occurred 13 or more years before, seems further to be establishing faith in the great oral tradition which allegedly developed among the followers of Socrates. Faith in this oral tradition was important because, as has been pointed out, we have nothing which was ever written by Socrates.

Apollodorus begins his report to his companions with these words, "Well, the tale of love was on this wise:—but perhaps I had better begin at the beginning, and endeavor to give you the exact words of Aristodemus." It seems the symposium (or banquet) was held at the Athenian home of Agathon on the occasion of his winning a prize at the theater with his first tragedy. A symposium, in modern times, is recognized as a gathering of men of some academic prominence in an atmosphere of sobriety for the purpose of a solemn exchange of views on a topic of common interest. The Greek symposium we are about to observe included the possibility of an exchange of views on an academic theme, but there was much more. There were flute girls, rich foods, strong wines, songs, laughter, fellowship, and on occasion, that which (in behalf of the sensitivities of the more delicately minded) we can call wenching. Except for the fact that some of the conversation at the symposium was of decided philosophic merit, the event wore aspects similar to some of the more well-rounded fraternity house parties known to occur on certain American college campuses.

The banquet opens with the usual respects paid to the host and to the prestigious Socrates who was late in arriving because he became lost in a "fit of abstraction" on the way. After the eating, drinking, and singing were well started, Pausanias, one of the group, arose to suggest that the rigors of drinking were already ravaging his person (evidently he had been to a previous party) and he asked Eryximachus, a physician who was present, to prescribe an activity which would give him time to recover. Eryximachus proposed they send the flute girl away and commence a succession of speeches in praise of love. All seemed to approve, especially Socrates who in his approbation cast something of a snide remark at his critic, Aristophanes, who was present and who, according to Socrates, should enjoy discussing love because his "whole concern is with Dionysius and Aphrodite."

PHAEDRUS. Socrates proposed that Phaedrus be the first speaker and Phaedrus began by "affirming that love is a mighty god and wonderful among gods and men." He then quoted Hesiod, the poet, and Parmenides, the philosopher, who taught men that love was the eldest and the greatest of the gods. Phaedrus indicated also that love was man's greatest benefactor.

This relates to mythological version of generation which was refined by the Platonists. The ancient pagans apparently thought that before earth, sea, and heaven were created all things wore a single aspect to which they gave the name of Chaos, "a confused and shapeless mass, nothing but dead weight in which, however, slumbered the seeds of all things." One of the gods began to organize this mass into rivers, bays, and seas. He raised up mountains, scooped out valleys, and formed fields, mountains, and fertile plains. He cleared the air, and stars appeared; and also, in time, there appeared fishes in the sea, birds in the air, and four-footed beasts on the land. Out of Chaos, therefore, was created order, and this order the Greeks called Cosmos.[3]

The refinements on this, which have been attributed to the Neoplatonists (chiefly Plotinus), consist of determining what intermediate steps occurred. First, there was creation of the Angelic Mind; second, the soul of the world; and third, the body of the world. These are steps relevant only to the extent they reveal that love was primarily the force (the god) which brought the Cosmos out of Chaos. Therefore, love was instrumental in creating the order which we call the world. Orderliness is beauty. Love, therefore, makes the

---

[3] Marsilio Ficino, *Commentary on Plato's Symposium* quoted in Albert Hofstadter and Richard Kuhns (ed.) *Philosophies of Art and Beauty* (New York: The Modern Library, Random House, Inc., 1964), p. 205.

disorderly orderly or the unbeautiful beautiful. The act of creating beauty is also considered wisdom because the ideas are said to occur in the Angelic Mind.

For these reasons it was appropriate for Phaedrus to acclaim love as "eldest of the gods" and "most wise," and he thereby nominated love as the god which out of chaos created the beauty men call order. His speech then turned to how love affects men. In essence, it makes them beautiful. It is the cause of their turning toward the good; it helps them toward fulfillment of the ideal of manhood. When a lover is observed by his beloved he is inspired to great things; such is the force of love. A lover in a dishonorable act is more pained at being discovered by his beloved than by any single thing. He cited cases where cowards became heroes, and even went on to say that any army composed of men who loved one another would be more valorous. So felicitous could be the effects of this love upon their manly attributes that "a mere handful . . . would overcome the world." According to Phaedrus, "courage which Homer said the gods breathe into the souls of heroes, love by its own nature infuses into the soul of the lover."

Phaedrus was not inclined to leave women out. He cited instances of nobility among women who, acting out of love, brought great honor to themselves, their families, and their cities. He concluded by attributing the decision of Achilles to stay and avenge Patroclus as the influence of the love each had for the other. It must have affected his audience deeply, for few stories could move the Greeks so profoundly as a recounting of the moment that Achilles resolved to confront Hector. He was forewarned that slaying Hector meant death for himself, but he made the choice to stay and fight; thus did love ennoble Achilles.

PAUSANIAS. The second speaker was Pausanias. He was critical of the form in which Phaedrus cast his argument, calling it indiscriminate. Pausanias was eager to account for the love which is founded on sexual attraction. Therefore, he invoked a dualism which, among the Platonists, seemed a favorite form of theorizing. Said Pausanias, "there are two loves and both seek to rule the world." One of them he called heavenly Aphrodite, and the other he called earthly, or common, Aphrodite. Heavenly Aphrodite was descended from Uranus, father of Zeus. She had no mother, for women have no part in this kind of love. On the other hand, common Aphrodite stemmed from one of

Zeus' exuberant and irresponsible sexual adventures with a mortal being.

The distinction in character between the two kinds of love is clear. Nothing joins the two. Common or earthly love is of women or of young boys. It is common, indiscriminate, and because it is sexual, it does not gain its end nobly. This love will do good or will do evil and has no power to discriminate between the two. Because the goddess was born of the union of male and female, this type of love is that in which women take part, and presumably for them, it is enough.

Heavenly Aphrodite is the force in life which moves the soul in the direction of the good. This love is not understood by the materialists who call these lovers madmen. But enlightened states understand them and permit lovers to do strange things. Those who know of the heavenly Aphrodite find that the actions of such a lover "have a grace which ennobles them." Such a love is an honorable thing. It is brought on by the sight of beauty which occurs in nature, art, or the soul of another man. This is the ecstatic Eros of a man who has transcended carnate relationships and has encountered beauty which has at its center the idea of good.

A man who loves in the spirit of this heavenly Aphrodite moves in the path of virtue. His service to his beloved is honorable in the sense that he performs it never for his own gain but to improve his beloved in wisdom or some other particular virtue. This kind of love a teacher may have for his student "and these two customs, one the love of youth and the other the practice of philosophy and virtue, ought to meet in one, and then the beloved may honorably indulge the lover."

Love in this sense is not a professional encounter governed by the usual ground rules of a material life. As Plato suggested in the *Phaedrus,* the true lover possesses the good in others by *having that good take possession of him.* One may give himself to a lover *because he is a good man.* It is virtuous and not vain for him to think that by this love his own soul will be improved. There is nobility in both the giving and the acceptance, for together there can be achieved a beautification and a transcendence of temporal life. The elements of this reasoning were preserved in the theology of the primitive Christian church and have remained alive in other religious expressions. This same reasoning remains still as an inspiring vision of how a student and teacher may be related.

The next speaker on the schedule was Aristophanes. However, Plato once again displayed a wayward and somwhat whimsical pen by afflicting Aristophanes with the embarrassment of having been seized by the hiccough. He had Aristophanes appeal to the physician Eryximachus, to either help him stop his hiccoughing or to speak in his place until the hiccough stopped on its own account. Eryximachus suggested that he would do both. He proposed a number of household remedies which would have Aristophanes alternately holding his breath, gargling, tickling his nose, and sneezing. Thus leaving Aristophanes to convulsions and cures, Eryximachus began to speak.

ERYXIMACHUS. He commenced by being critical of the ending which Pausanias supplied. As a physician Eryximachus was evidently distrustful of solutions outside the physical domain. He offered to amend this deficiency. He held that Pausanias was correct in distinguishing between the two kinds of love, but his own art informed him that this double love was not an affection of the soul. It is to be found in the body of man and animals and in all the productions of the earth. Eryximachus then presented a materialistic analysis of the nature of love, and, although he made full and appropriate reference to the heavenly myths, there is no mistaking the Ionian influences in his thought. He even went so far as to quote Heraclitus, although he found it necessary to correct him.

Eryximachus offered a theory that the two loves are decidedly unlike. He called one the desire of the healthy and the other the desire of the diseased. There are in the body good and healthy elements— these he would encourage. There are also bad elements, the elements of disease—these he would discourage. This, said Eryximachus, is what a physician does. Knowledge of medicine is knowledge of the loves and desires of the body. The best physician is he who can separate foul love from fair and convert the former to the latter. He must know how to eradicate one and implant the other.

He declared that the most hostile are the most opposite such as hot and cold, bitter and sweet, moist and dry. The artist knows how these lovers are blended in temperance. Temperance is the basis of not only medicine but other arts as well. Musical notes may be discordant, and various musical instruments may have sounds which are disunited. The art of the musician is to reconcile these elements in harmony and unity. This is what the musician brings to the opposing elements in music and the physician brings to contending elements in health.

Harmony in the seasons of the year brings forth health in plants and animals. A similar kind of balance keeps the heavenly bodies rotating in their place. Thus, man must reverence harmony in all of his actions. The harmonious love is the perfect love because the effects of this love are good. The harmonized love is the greatest power and the source of all that is beautiful. For this love brings prosperity to all things and destroys no things.

The real dissent of Eryximachus from the theories of the previous speakers is somewhat obscured. This, some authorities claim, suggests the ambivalence of Plato toward the materialistic point of view. Plato evidently did not like it well enough to base his metaphysical system upon it. On the other hand, he seemed not able to overlook its basic appeal.

Eryximachus argued that love was that which blended the forces of the world into a beautiful, productive, and sustaining environment. If he took seriously the comments made by his friends about the soul, he failed to show it. The physician was satisfied that love existed in the world of the senses. Why did Plato pass these sentiments through his lips? The modern commentator can only guess that as a teacher Plato thought he owed his students and his readers opportunity to consider another point of view, or perhaps, on the other hand, he wanted to be certain they knew he was aware of the other point of view.

ARISTOPHANES. Having completed his remarks Eryximachus turned to Aristophanes and noted that he was at last rid of the hiccough. Aristophanes admitted that it was gone but not until he had applied the sneezing. And with a teasing reference to that which Eryximachus had just uttered, and apparently to the merriment of the others, Aristophanes said, "I wonder whether the harmony of the body has love of such noises and ticklings, for I no sooner applied the sneezing and I was cured." Eryximachus, evidently stung, warned Aristophanes that he, the physician, would listen carefully to the playwright's forthcoming speech in order to obtain laughter at Aristophanes' expense. Aristophanes replied to the effect that before finishing he would, without help from Eryximachus, be laughed at by everyone; and then he proceeded to prove his point.[4]

---

[4] G. M. A. Grube, *Plato's Thought* (Boston: Beacon Press, 1958), p. 99. See also: Irving Sevinger, *The Nature of Love, Plato to Luther* (New York: Random House, 1966), p. 69. Many commentaries agree that Plato was simply true to Aristophanes' style, a farce with broad serious undercurrents.

Aristophanes declared that at one time the sexes were not two but three (because the sun, moon, and earth are three). They were man, woman, and man-woman. Now these three sorts of creatures looked alike and were called androgynous. This primeval man was round, his back and sides forming a circle. He had four hands, four feet, and one head with two faces looking out in opposite directions. He could walk upright as men now do, and he could roll over and over at a great pace when he wanted to travel fast. These creatures had great powers and growing ambitions, and the time came to pass when they made an attack on the gods. They dared to scale the heavens, threatening to lay hands upon the gods, and their insolence became intolerable. What to do?

Zeus was equal to the occasion. To "humble their pride and improve their manners" he decided to cut them in half in order that they were required to walk upright on two legs, and, said he, "should their arrogance continue, I will split them again and they shall hop about on a single leg." Thereupon, he executed his plan and "cut them in two like a sorb apple which is halved for pickling." He gave the face and neck half a turn so the creature could survey the effects of the cut. He pulled the skin across, made appropriate repairs, and turned the parts of generation around to the front. From this time the halved creatures sowed their seeds into each other rather than into the grass as hitherto was their practice.

Now the parts are free to multiply and inhabit the earth. But they suffer the anxieties and pain of incomplete animals. Each half yearns for that from which it was separated. Those halves which were once part of an androgynous which was male on both sides tend to cleave to other males. These, of course, are the more valiant of the two remaining sexes. Those who were part of an androgynus which was double female, find greater association with that sex. Finally, those who were part of the creature that was man on one side and woman on the other are attracted to the opposite sex. It is out of the unions of these latter two that the race continues itself.

But the yearning goes on—each man is a half-soul who wanders the face of the earth searching eagerly for his other half. Rarely does he ever find it, but in a few rare cases soul mates discover each other. This is as close as the agony, which men call love, ever comes to fulfillment. And even then it cannot be complete because the breech cannot be closed. Love, therefore, is a yearning to be whole again, a quest to merge once again into an original nature. Aristophanes asserted that should soul mates meet, neither of the pair would hesitate before a prospect of melting into one another, thus becoming one instead of two.

Having made this point, Aristophanes then exhorted his companions to greater piety, for the danger remains that Zeus will carry out his threat to bisect man once again, thus rendering his original nature into quarters instead of halves. Aristophanes left the confusion this would cause to be explained by the rich and varied imaginations of those who heard him. His prescription for man, therefore, was to avoid evil, remain friends of the gods, and to seek openly for the mate which would enable him to return to his primeval nature. This, said he, is the basis upon which our race can be happy. Then with an appeal to Eryximachus to not ridicule him but to take him seriously, Aristophanes lapsed into silence.

The myth which Aristophanes told could have originated in any of several primitive sources. And among such people it has appeal. It accounts for both homosexual and heterosexual love, and as some claim for psychoanalysis, it helps man with the guilt feelings he seems often to associate with his emergence on earth. Like Adam, the androgynous was guilty of "original sin" and, as in the doctrine of the fall, the half-creature which remains has his unaccountable yearning explained to him. The myth has its uses. It is also found to be of some philosophic merit in the sense that love can be explained as an effort to achieve wholeness. The myth of the androgynus does not dwell on sexuality. It is an innate desire to be reunited with one's self. The myth seems to demote the role of sex in love to just another natural function. Certainly any biological fulfillment which stems from successful sexual ventures in no way answers to the yearning which the myth holds to be part of every man. Love is the need to recover that which is lost, the pain of incompleteness. Sexuality may or may not be derived from this. In any case, it is clearly secondary to it.

AGATHON. The fifth speaker was Agathon, the host. Before his discourse began he exchanged sentiments with Socrates on the differences between this audience and the great audience at the theater who were captivated by his play. Socrates seemed to want to make something out of the kind of audience which had approved the artistic efforts put forward by Agathon, but the latter was wary of him. "Do you think, Socrates," said Agathon, "that my head is so full of the theater as to not know how much more formidable to a man of sense a few good judges are than many fools?"[5] But Phaedrus interrupted, begging Agathon to speak. Thus for a time at least, he was spared from the Socratic blade.

In Agathon's speech the god Love is praised on his own account. In writing words for the mouth of Agathon, who was a poet, Plato displayed his own poetic power. The words and phrases depicted a fair god, forever young, who was himself good and beautiful and because he was good and beautiful was the cause of goodness and beauty in others. Agathon called him soft, fair, just, temperate, courageous; a poet, and a maker of poets, an artist and maker of artists, and a creator of order. Before Love came the empire of the gods was rife with contention and conflict. Love set the empire in order, made peace in heaven, and brings peace to earth. He empties men of their disaffections and fills them with affection. He "makes them meet together in banquets such as these."

In a final soaring summary Agathon declared:

> . . . he is our lord—who sends courtesy and sends away discourtesy, who gives kindness ever and never gives unkindness; the friend of the good, the wonder of the wise, the amazement of the gods; desired by those who have no part in him, and precious to those who have better part in him; parent of delicacy, luxury, desire, fondness, softness, grace, regardful of the good, regardless of the evil; in every word, work, wish, fear—savior, pilot, comrade, helper; glory of gods and men, leader best and brightest; in whose footsteps let every man follow, sweetly singing in his honor and joining in that sweet strain with which love charms the souls of god and men.

At the end of this there was a general cheer, and Socrates looked at Eryximachus and said, "Tell me, son of Acumenus, was there not reason in my fears? And was I not a true prophet when I said that Agathon would make a wonderful creation, and that I should be in a strait?" Socrates tried to excuse himself, speaking first on the ground that he could not give satisfaction following so rich a discourse as that which they had just heard and, second, on the ground that he had not understood the compact. When pressed for clarification of his latter concern, Socrates responded to the effect that the speakers had been praising imaginary attributes of greatness and goodness, saying of

---

[5] Note Plato's reservations about the theater.

Love that "he is all this" and "the cause of all that." Socrates declared it was not in his nature to compose hymns of this kind and begged to be absolved of his promise to speak.

On the other hand he said, if the audience wished to hear the truth about Love, he was ready to speak in his own manner. The request was immediately made that he do so, whereupon he indicated that he would like to start by asking Agathon a few questions. Agathon agreed. With his usual courtesy and deference, Socrates complimented Agathon for choosing to speak first on the nature of Love and then later on his (Love's) works. He then asked Agathon questions about the assertions Agathon had made on the nature of Love. He wanted to know if Love was of something or of nothing. When Agathon agreed that Love was of something, Socrates proceeded to question him. As the dialogue proceeded it soon became evident that Socrates was applying various elements of formal logic as a means of testing the truth of Agathon's assertion that Love is beautiful and good. Finally, Socrates invoked the principle of contradiction to show Agathon's fallacy. The dialogue consummated as follows:

Socrates: . . . the admission has already been made that Love is of something which a man wants and has not?
Agathon: True.
Socrates: Then Love wants and has not beauty?
Agathon: Certainly.
Socrates: And would you call that beautiful which wants and has not beauty?
Agathon: Certainly not.
Socrates: Then would you still say Love is beautiful?
Agathon: I fear that I did not understand what I was saying.
Socrates: You made a good speech, Agathon, but there is yet one question which I would fain ask. Is not the good also the beautiful?
Agathon: Yes.
Socrates: Then in wanting the beautiful, Love wants also the good?
Agathon: I cannot refute you, Socrates. Let us assume what you say is true.
Socrates: Say rather, beloved Agathon, that you cannot refute the truth, for Socrates is easily refuted.

THE WISDOM OF DIOTIMA. Having demolished Agathon, who

was at first so enthusiastically applauded by all of the company, Socrates was the master of the moment. All eyes and ears were attuned to his every movement and word. He was in a position which every real teacher envies. In the vernacular of our present day, we would say that he had the *undivided attention of his class*. But a teacher who gets into this extreme advantage had better have something to say to his class. Socrates did. He proceeded to rehearse a tale which he called *The Wisdom of Diotima*. And who can say this wily old prolocutor was not escalating the attention of his hearers even more by saying he was about to profess that taught to him by a strange woman from Mantinea who was his "instructress in the art of love."

Socrates indicated that his words to Diotima were similar to those of Agathon. Socrates said that he told Diotima that Love was a great god who was beautiful. She then took the same means that he had taken with Agathon to show that Love has not and wants beauty and, therefore, cannot be beautiful. He then asked her if Love was, therefore, foul. "Hush," she cried, "must that be foul which is not fair?" She pointed out there was a middle between such things as foul and fair, wise and ignorant, etc. By allegorical reasoning she demonstrated for him that love was not a god at all but a spirit in both God and man who mediates between the two and is the agency by which God and man are communicated. Love takes the prayers and sacrifices of men across to God and brings the replies of God back to man.

She told Socrates that love could not be a god (or be God), but that it was the power which drew men to that which was godly. God is good, wise, and beautiful. Therefore, love is that which exists in man which shows itself by the adoration of goodness, wisdom, and beauty. (These three words form a trinity; in the Platonic sense they are assumed to be three ways of talking about one thing—namely, the good.) Thus, it is incorrect to say that love is beautiful or that God is Love. Love is not a property either of mortality or divinity. Rather, it mediates between the two, and its character is bodiless, ethereal, and wholly transcendental. It is fulfilled in man at the highest levels through the exercise of his reason.

But this answer, Socrates said, did not help him understand the uses of love in men. He wanted Diotima to move from the realms of pure reason to practical reason. In a practical sense how does this love operate in men? How is it seen? When a man wants beauty, what is it that he wants? And when a man comes to possess beauty, what is it that he has? Diotima, he said, had no ready answer for him, but bade him to put the word good in place of the word beauty. His questions then became: When a man wants the good, what is it that he wants? And when a man has the good, what is it that he has?

Again, by allegorical reasoning, using as her example the creative arts, Diotima demonstrated for Socrates that anything which passes from nonbeing into being acquires at its moment of conception a craving for immortality. Everything apparently dies, but nothing wishes to. In every mortal creature the principles of conception and generation are immortal. The struggles and sufferings of human life are animated by the desire for immortality. Man, the creature, finds himself in a world of material change, but this world goes on and he, apparently, does not. His body, composed of the elements of nature, is destined to be resolved back into those elements. Soon, his being becomes infused with concern for its continuance. His physical beauty comes, and with advancing years, begins to fade. How shall he minister to his being which by its own nature cries out for its continuance? Thus, to men, the universal good is that which will bestow the quality of immortality to their being.

It is not difficult to infer from this that Socrates was suggesting that a man is made happier by the advancement of any prospect of his immortality. At the seat of his being he would declare this to be good. Now if beauty is part of the good or is the good itself, a man may find beauty in anything which advances his immortal nature or reminds him of its prospects. Thus, each soul, in the interests of its own immortality, hungers for beauty and wishes to create it and yearns to be part of it.

Socrates continued by giving several examples which Diotima offered. The highest form of immortality is that achieved by the soul who writes laws and creates states. The greatest beauty a man can produce is a condition of order in which man can live in a state of harmony (which is in itself beautiful). She cited the case of Solon, "the revered father of Athenian law" and the case of Lycurgus of Lacedaemonia. Perhaps on a lesser level of creativity and beauty are the poets such as Homer and Hesiod who brought immortality to themselves through the beauty of their works. She told of the great heroes whose names lived on in the words and thoughts of the generations which followed them because their sacrifices of life were so beautiful that the quality of immortality came to their being which by its beauty was and is eternal. Finally, lesser men who are not so creative in their souls create through their bodies by taking to themselves women to produce offspring which will carry their names and will preserve them in memory when the time comes that their bodies will no longer sustain their being. Even animals experience agony and passion in their procreation and they gladly hunger and suffer in order to maintain their young. At the approach of predatory danger they will defend these offspring to the uttermost. All is done so that something may go on, something may continue. But all procreation, whether the offspring is a law, a poem, a statue, or a child, must be in beauty and in the spirit of creation. It is a divine thing. She said:

> Beauty, then, is the destiny or goddess of parturition, who presides at birth, and therefore, when approaching beauty, the conceiving power is propitious, and diffusive, and benign, and begets and bears fruit: at the sight of ugliness she frowns and contracts and has a sense of pain, and turns away, and shrivels up, and not without a pang refrains from conception.

Love, therefore, is the sovereign urge to create beauty. This urgency animates the soul.[6] It is not a uniform quality in men. Those whose souls are highly galvanized know greater agony and greater ecstasy. Their sensitivities are said to be deeper and their personal complexities greater. For this above any other is the life which a man should live. By this is meant the contemplation of beauty in the absolute; such a beauty, once beheld, would make the seemingly enchanted appeals of gold, maidens, and youth unworthy of attention of the philosopher. One would be content to be with them and to look at them. But Diotima said:

> If a man had eyes to see true beauty—the divine beauty, I mean pure, clean, and unalloyed, not clogged with the pollutions of mortality and all the colors and vanities of human life— thither looking, and holding converse the true beauty simple and divine . . . in that communion only, beholding beauty with the eye of the mind, he will be ennobled to bring forth not images of beauty, but realities (for he has hold not of an image but of a reality) and bringing forth the nourishing true virtue to become the friend of God and immortal, if any man may.

---

[6] Ficino, op. cit., pp. 222-224, 237.

Man will not find a greater ally to his purpose in life than love. But he must understand it. Should he waste his desire to create on mere sensation, or on the base, the ignoble, or the vulgar? If he dissipates his creative urges, and brings forth only that which is ugly, evil, or destructive, he has in the ultimate sense wasted his substance. These will be only waxing and waning, dissolution and decay. Socrates ended his speech by reminding the company that the words he spoke were the words of Diotima and he believed them true. When he had done speaking the audience applauded.

ALCIBIADES. The climax of the *Symposium* had passed; that which remained was anticlimax. Why did Plato not stop? What, after having put forward his definition of love, decided him that there was more to be said? And why, above all men, did he choose as his narrator the corrupt Alcibiades? It is possible that having said what love was Plato found it important to record what it was not. Or perhaps he did not wish to let so meaningful a human concern rest on the ethereal, abstract, and somewhat uncertain notions of mortality. Perhaps he wanted to clarify the applications of his ideas to specific aspects of human relationships. If these are the purposes he had in mind, he certainly achieved them.

Alcibiades had been out on the town and drinking heavily. Somewhere and at some time in the midst of his revels, he decided to pay a call on Agathon to congratulate him for his success in the theater. So shortly after Socrates finished speaking he burst in on the scene. The arrival of so colorful and forceful a personality in a state of inebriation would throw any gathering into an uproar, and this is what happened. The exchanges were mixed, some jovial, and some barbed. But in the end it was decided that Alcibiades should speak on the theme of the evening. Being the sort he was, he took up the challenge, warning the company that in his drunken state he would speak unrestrainedly, truthfully, and without the inhibitions which engrace polite conversation.

Evidently, Socrates was a problem for Alcibiades. He loved Socrates, and were not he (Alcibiades) so popular and in such demand in the gay social circles of Athens he would have been content to be a student of Socrates. (Every graduate professor knows of the ostensible graduate student who would study under him if he had time to give from other pursuits.) There was no man for whom Alcibiades had greater admiration. So great it was that he devoted the whole of his speech to what he called the "praise of Socrates." He revealed, in some detail, how he became enamored of Socrates and attempted to seduce him, but found that his physical advances were met with comments or questions which diverted him away from matters of the flesh to matters of internal beauty. Alcibiades asserted that he was at first annoyed (for Alcibiades was considered very fair and physically attractive as a youth); then he was disappointed; and finally, he was intrigued.

He claimed that even though Socrates' face resembled the mask of Silenus, Socrates was the most beautiful of men. His words and thoughts were greater than the greatest of orators. Beauty of the flesh and the glories of wealth and honor were of no account to him. Alcibiades told how Socrates on the field of battle had saved the lives of others and stood aside when Alcibiades himself received a prize for valor which was really earned by Socrates. He confessed how he and certain other young men of Athens had tried, without success, to corrupt him. They failed.

Alcibiades indicated that the failure in his relations with Socrates was a failure to understand the nature of friendship. Friends exchange beauty for beauty. Alcibiades, who in the flesh was beautiful, and Socrates, who was not, had difficulty in consummating their friendship. The reason for this difficulty was that Socrates had many beauties to offer and Alcibiades had few to return. He found great irony in this and would like to have stayed with Socrates in order that beauty could grow within him, but the appeal of the crowd was too eloquent, and he was too weak to resist. However, his passion for Socrates remained, and he seems to have found it difficult to keep his hands from Socrates' person. This was the only level of love which Alcibiades knew. It is a level which manifests in physical contacts only. Alcibiades to his regret found himself incapable of higher love, and in his intoxicated state (*in vino veritas!*) he confessed this truth to the company.

THE SYMPOSIUM AND AMERICAN EDUCATION. Now what implications does all of this have for those who teach American children? Plato associated love with life purpose. America is a nation suffering a crisis of purpose, and any human attribute which relates to purpose holds a powerful relevance to the work of teachers and teaching. Any question of purpose includes in its range of subject matter *the nature of the good*. And in the *Symposium* Plato speaks of the good as something which can be possessed.

Love, to the Platonist, is not a recognition or surrender to human deficiencies. Instead it is a struggle inherent to the organism itself, a struggle to overcome these deficiencies. It is the rigors which this struggle entails and the rapture which stands as its reward which inclines Plato to write as if it were bereft of interpersonal feelings. Thus the criticism that Platonic love does not permit warm human relationships is frequently heard. However, there is sufficient evidence in the *Symposium* itself to put this complaint to rest. The Platonists were not disposed to deride or disdain physical relations between humans except in so far as disdain may be *implied* by the high value assigned to acts of beautification through the creative propensities inherent in all men.

Today the American man on the street associates love with sex alone—and why shouldn't he? Has there been a concerted effort of any kind to confront him with a broader, more developed idea? No; on the contrary, he is almost continuously urged to think that love is sexuality alone. The basic appeal of sex is used to sell all kinds of products; it is almost a universal constituent of every form of fiction; it seems to increasingly dominate the theater arts; and the various fashions in clothes and cosmetics invite exaggerated appraisal. The prospect that man and woman, man and man, or woman and woman, could sustain an intense friendship which does not have sexuality as a base or as an object is simply not accepted in many American communities. A Platonic friendship is almost a term of derision. Few Americans admit that it is a possibility.

This cynicism stems from the inability of this man on the street to appreciate that such possibilities do exist, not only for others, but for him as well. If Plato was anywhere near being right about the human values developed in the *Symposium*, then this typical American has been denied access to part of his own life. Or, to put it more gently, there are prospects of life that have never been opened to him. This failure can be attributed to institutions which tried to educate him, his family, his school, his church (if any), and the various elements of mass communication media to which he is constantly exposed. Thus do institutions withhold the forms by which civil men establish inner order.

Now the problem is bigger than simply being deprived of Platonic friendships. Men have, it seems, an increasingly impoverished view of the work they do in the world. Work, as an act, is performed for the material benefits which follow work. Many men and women sustain themselves in a job simply by the thoughts of the pay—the money and the benefits.[7] The job in itself means next to nothing. They do not know or sense the surging need to create, to achieve the good. Again, on the contrary, they are often discouraged by labor organizations (some of the less enlightened) from *giving themselves to the good.*

We spend a great part of life doing some kind of work. If this work does not ennoble a man then it must debase him. The fact that he earns money while doing such work may redeem it on his scale of values. But any amount of money cannot buy back wasted time and opportunity. Creative work need not be the arts in the conventional sense. A waitress, a delivery boy, or one who provides home services can do this work with a quality, a pride, and a sense of satisfaction which fulfills a Platonic paradigm. A man who puts a roof on a house, a heating plant in a building, or print in a newspaper can feel "the wisdom of Diotima" in the sense that there is something of his self that goes into the work which he does, and something of his immortal self which comes out of it.

What does this mean? Many, in fact all, of the superb technologies we have today were developed by men who knew or sensed the ideal workmanship or craftsmanship related to the idea of good. These technologies they managed to communicate to others; and, they, to even others. Along the way thousands of men whose work was beautiful became immortal by the buildings they built, the fabrics they made, and the skills they developed. The immortality is incarnated daily as these skills are reapplied or made the basis of even higher skills. It is all a part of the same thing. A man who spades his garden to-day is connected by a long chain to remote ancestors who were struggling to understand the use of levers. The shovel itself, its form and material substance, reflect beauty which has been created and which has immortalized those who had a part in it. The good and the beautiful can make work a thing of great humane worth.[8]

All this and much more is implied by the words which Plato placed in the speech of Socrates. Each of the preliminary speakers contributed something and Alcibiades served to clarify something. The *Symposium* itself is a great work—certainly one which needs more attention today. But often this attention is withheld because it reflected a tendency to depreciate the female role in life and because some of the conversation seems, frankly, homosexual. However, in modern

---

[7] Phenix, *op. cit.*, p. 94.
[8] *Ibid.*, p. 105-106.

times we can dismiss both of these allegations on the grounds of cultural differences. In antiquity the male was thought to contain all the seminal powers of life. Now that the full genetic partnership of male and female has been revealed, the rational basis for masculine bigotry has been dissolved. Plato, himself, must have sensed this because in the speech of Pausanias he wrote admiringly of women, and in presenting the climactic speech, he used as his dramatic source a woman named Diotima.

On the overtones of homosexuality, the careful reader will note that Alcibiades was rejected by Socrates, thereby making one of the central points of the book. It was a point that had to be made and Plato chose the right way to make it. Were he writing for modern culture wherein heterosexual relations are clearly the vogue, he may have put a woman in the role of Alcibiades. That he used a handsome young man instead of a beautiful woman gives us cultural insights which have been made tenable by other evidence of life in classical antiquity. Did Plato approve of homosexuality? Indeed, no. He denounces it, and in the *Laws* he would have the lawgiver enact statutes against it.

Fortunately, modern students can rise above the cultural differences to grip the transcending ideas which Plato offers. This is one of the possibilities in modern life for which the modern academic profession can congratulate itself. However, being capable of rising above cultural differences to an appropriate level of abstraction, and doing it, are not the same, and the contemporary view of the meaning of love is a case in point. Institutions of education must work to enlarge the prospective lives of those whom we educate, not to reduce them. Reduction can be accomplished by a failure to expose wholesome possibilities for being. The Platonic arguments are powerful instruments for this purpose. They should no longer be unused by American public education.

ORDEALS OF IDEALS

THE BURLESQUE OF IDEALS. One thing indispensable to burlesque is an ideal. Without an ideal a burlesque is meaningless. There is really nothing to burlesque; words and gestures to that end are ludicrous. However, given an ideal, the burlesque takes on meaning. It plays upon various public feelings about the ideal which is mockingly portrayed. If we take notice of the ideals which are burlesqued in modern life and how the burlesque is received, we can learn much about the status of ideals. Clues of this kind demonstrate the ends and values of society which are esteemed and those which are not.

To accept or enjoy a burlesque a man must know the ideal well, but not too well. He must know enough to appreciate what it is the burlesque artist is attempting to parody, but he must not feel so attached to the ideal that the burlesque offends him. For example, cartoonists often caricature well known personalities or ideas. To understand or enjoy the cartoon one must know the person or idea well enough to recognize who or what is being ridiculed. Certainly a caricature must fail at the first level if its principal figure is not recognizable. When a cartoonist renders a derisive caricature of the President of the United States he may wish to portray him as a simpleton at work but he also wants everyone to know that it is the President, so he exaggerates the physical features by which the man as a person is known. Most Americans do not object to satirical caricatures of their President, but occasionally one appears which desecrates the office. Most Americans object to this regardless of their personal attachment to the President because the Presidency is a widely accepted symbol of our nationhood. Nationhood is an ideal and most Americans still feel deeply about the ideal of America.

Often a comedian burlesques a performance of the ballet. Almost everyone is sufficiently familiar with ballet to sense what is going on. They have seen a ballet in ideal form, so nearly everyone will think it funny and enjoy it. However, this may not hold true for lovers of the ballet. Depending on how it is done, the ballet lover may find such a burlesque a desecration of the ideal and resent it deeply. A burlesque of ballet, therefore, would be a risky thing to offer an audience of ballet enthusiasts. But this same audience might applaud a burlesque of college professors or five star generals.

Burlesque at the level of portrayal can be acceptable. No one objects to a drawing of Uncle Sam. In cartoons he often appears as a well-meaning, hard working, nice guy, who just blundered into one more global embarrassment and is trying to discover a way out. After all, this is how things often seem. The burlesque in this case helps our state of mind by showing that important matters can have a humorous aspect. It helps to gain perspective. In this way the cartoonist by his outlandish expressions serves the good. However, malicious or capricious desecration is something else. No one accepts desecration of an ideal except those indifferent or opposed to the ideal which is desecrated. Often a publicist or performer who has done this is taken to task. He is accused of bad taste or worse, but this happens only when there are many who are devoted to the ideal he has abominated.

Therefore, there are two ways in which the ideal can excite human feelings. One is in its realization, and the other is in its abomination. We need to pay attention to both. Few men have not experienced the joy which comes from the realization of an ideal. The regenerating inspiration of the Virgin Mother has two sources for its beauty. One is the ideal of purity and the other is the ideal of Universal Motherhood. Taken together with others these comprise the plenary ideal of Womanhood. To all except literalistic Christians, the influence is allegorical; however, an ideal does not require authentication by the standards of historical criticism. The vision of Womanhood inherent in the symbol of the Virgin Mother has been the theme of countless works of art.[1] Its colloquial vitality merges with other visions and symbols and infuses the whole with benign tenderness and solicitude. Thus conjured is the ideal of Womanhood, probably the most civilizing influence in western man and unquestionably the most formidable obstacle to his degeneracy.

She is the guardian of dignity, the custodian of sentiment whose personal grace in moving and speaking bestows beauty on both object and word. She has a cultivated sense of the arts; her personal relations are constantly tempered in affection, yet she never neglects the fine

---

[1] George Santayana, *The Sense of Beauty* (New York: The Dover Publications, Inc., 1955), p. 189.

edge of her animal intuition. Her sexuality is authentic and acknowledged, never subdued and never amplified. She is loyal to mate, devoted to offspring, benevolent to stranger, and bears the anxieties and pain natural to her sex in uncomplaining solitude. She is an ideal, matched in the person of any woman loved by man or child and in the dreams of men and children who have no woman to love. She is an ideal; she is the standard by which men know goodness not only in women, but in all things with which she deals, including men.

When conceived in this spirit the idea of Womanhood is an experience of beauty. The female body is beautiful; this is a source of beauty lost from Christian expressions of the ideal. By beauty of body is meant the art of Praxiteles and not the distorted phantasies of professional pornographers and the sexually obsessed consumers of their travesties. These aspects of womanhood are external and temporal. Their relation to the ideal is perfunctory and incidental. The authentic woman invites her beholders to contemplate her inner qualities which are of the eternal rather than temporal order. Therefore, the physical representation of woman is of an ideal. One must be educated in ideality to have the experience in beauty which comes from acquaintance with a woman who incarnates the ideal. To those not educated in ideality an experience with the ideal of womanhood is meaningless; more, it is resented.

THE LOW BURLESQUE OF WOMANHOOD. Therefore, those who do not appreciate the ideal delight, indeed revel, in its abomination. Thus, the appetite is born for the low burlesque of Womanhood. In this way the ideal of Woman is widely corrupted in American life. There is reason to think that it is more widely corrupted than any other. There are both men *and* women who enjoy the low burlesque of Womanhood. There are women who make their lives and professions a low burlesque of Womanhood. Men and women who pack the bars and restaurants enjoy the abomination of the ideal, because, not participating in its beauty, they resent the strictures the ideal of Woman places on animal license.

This, and not the relish of a shower room scene, is what packs them in. The body of Woman is an object of art. Those who wish to witness its beauty need not go far. Mere exposure of the female form, however, does nothing to the ideal, and it is the ideal that must be derogated in burlesque. Notice that in a burlesque of Womanhood the performer first appears on stage as a lady of fashion and refinement.

This fixes the ideal in the mind of the audience. Then, of course, she proceeds to a low burlesque. Those who enjoy low burlesque applaud the degradation of women. Such a burlesque of Womanhood makes it possible for a man to lay down the burdens of manhood and revel in animality. Again, it is not true that those who delight in the low burlesque of Woman are unaware of the ideal. The simple truth is they have not risen beyond the first level of abstraction. *If one were to pass among the predominantly male audience, pausing by each to suggest that the female performer be replaced by his own mother, daughter, wife, or sister, the response would be angry.* But the respondent would not understand the deep base of his own anger.

Why would he be offended? In the early paragraphs of his *Essay on History,* Emerson proclaimed, "The creation of a thousand forests is in one acorn." He went on to point out that all of the great civilizations of the world "be folded already in the first man." In his essay, *The Oversoul,* this same philosopher asserted that "Our being flows into us from a single source." Plato might think of this source as the array of archetypes which include the ultimate idea of Manhood and Womanhood. Thus, in the burlesque of the ideal, the performer is degrading that part of a man's sister, mother, wife, or daughter which *is* Woman. The low burlesque of Woman, therefore, diminishes every woman. It is not an experience in beauty, nor is it a beautiful obscenity. It is not a girl being "naughty." Usually, it is a shamefully unskilled, performer demonstrating that the ideal of Womanhood is a sham, a fake, something to be ridiculed.

If those who celebrate such performances have even a limited capacity for abstraction they can be brought to see that the performer *is* his wife, daughter, mother, *and* sister. With such recognition he would soon feel an inner urging to take his business elsewhere. In a short while the consequences of this would bring such performances to an end. Happily, the end would come without the very dubious benefits of raids, arrests, and courtroom pyrotechnics which feature saucy harridans posing as heroines of man's endless struggles against suppression.

Ideals such as the ideal of Womanhood restrain while they reward. Their most decisive qualities are aesthetic. They appeal to our sense of beauty, and when the aesthetic qualities begin to warm the consciousness one begins to discover the richer, fuller, a life the human animal can never realize. Lest there be misunderstanding, the idea of Woman does not represent withdrawal from life. Woman is not a

china doll. One of the most vivid and well known personalities in
modern literature is D. H. Lawrence's (Constance) Chatterly. Lady
Chatterly did not corrupt the idea of Woman. Her story demonstrates
the abuses women often suffer at the hands of silly and oppressive
institutions. She emerges clothed in dignity despite her journey through
a "four-letter" environment.

Turning to the contemporary arts we are further instructed in the
corruption of Womanhood by numerous works of fiction which seem
to allege that women themselves prefer to be brutalized. "When you
go to women," Nietzsche once declared, "take your whip with you."
This eagerness of philosophy and fiction to degrade Woman accelerates
the descent from the ideal. But the animal performance of female
wrestlers remains a curiosity as long as the ideal they corrupt is
somewhere to be noted and resented by those who have only a partial
sense of its real beauty.

A rich and prosperous industry has developed from the sale of
magazines devoted to this kind of thing. In recent years it has grown
to be called an empire. Probably those photographs of young women
in unnatural and unbeautiful postures are intended to idealize sexuality in Woman. This ideal is antithetical to the civilizing ideal which
has nourished order in western institutions. It goes beyond low
burlesque by establishing erotic standards for human relationships.
Journalism of this kind is not so much a burlesque of Woman as it is
an effort to redefine Woman. One such magazine which seems now to
regard itself as an institution has worked out a theory of Womanhood
which makes her an instrument of man's pleasure. Presumably Manhood serves women in the same way. It would be a mistake to think of
this Ovidian reality as merely a low burlesque of women. This burlesque is of philosophy itself. The desperate condition of our idea of
Woman and of the low estate of modern philosophy is revealed in the
fact that this degenerate idea of Woman and its accompanying parody
on philosophy are taken seriously by so great a number of young men
and women who have had the best that western institutions can offer.

THE BURLESQUE OF FREEDOM. As the strumpet in a bawdy
show does her work in the name of Woman, so the anarchist does his
work in the name of Freedom. Again, it is low burlesque. Like the
degraders of Womanhood, the degraders of Freedom win a following
among those who have only a limited knowledge of the idea. Their
enjoyment of the burlesque is countered by the anguish it gives to

lovers of Freedom who have given study to the ideal and recognize its human potencies. Ironically, it is the lover of Freedom who must, in the spirit of his own ideal, countenance its burlesque even though he does so in despair.

An episode in anarchy cannot last long. As an *annual* which grows wildly in the field, it has its season, casts off its seeds, and dies. When a new season arrives the seeds from the former anarchy long dormant in the ground germinate, sprout, raise up stalks, cast off seeds, and die. Anarchy is not Freedom, and a weed is not a tree. Anarchy has no idea and, therefore, raises up no institution. But it grows up wild and infests institutions consecrated to Freedom. Anarchy flourishes where the idea of Freedom is not understood. Thus, does this low burlesque of Freedom win its following.

The idea of Freedom may be approached from either one of two major aspects, personal freedom or societal freedom. Within the past two centuries existentialist writers have dealt extensively with the issue of personal freedom. In general, they have asserted that freedom is the fundamental condition necessary for human action. Freedom is achieved by the act of *nihilating* "being in itself" for "being for itself." Essentially, nihilation means that man discovers he is a "self" and not an "object." He thereby becomes fully conscious of his self-existence, and recognizes that he is the source of his own meaning, and the only such source possible.[2]

Personal meaning to the existentialist is accomplished by personal choice. By the feat of nihilation a man establishes that he has no predetermined essence. The way is open for choice, and by the accumulation of choices *a man establishes his essence*. His essence is subject to change with each new choice. It is proper, therefore, to say that a man's essence is incomplete until his life is over and he can no longer choose. Thus did the wretched Sidney Carton change drastically his essence by his final choice in Dickens' epic, *Tale of Two Cities*. His decision to go beneath the falling knife in the place of the fleeing Darnay was a free choice. It was a human *act*. By it, his essence came to be vastly different than it was. Freedom exists when each man comes to terms with the fact that he has the same power of choice as every other man.

But a choice includes consequence! When one chooses, he accepts

---

[2] Jean Paul Sartre, *Existentialism* (New York: Philosophical Library, 1947), p. 18.

all of the consequences of his choice. One cannot act upon a moral choice without at the same time accepting the consequences inbedded therein. One does not inflict his will upon the operations of his fellow men and then rightly claim amnesty. Such a claim, whether granted or not, deprives the original act of its meaning and adds nothing of worth to the general cultivation of institutions. Indeed, an appeal from guilt is an indication that those involved in such conduct have not performed the feat of nihilation and that they concur in the social judgment that the act was in fact immoral. To ask to be excused is to confess wrongdoing. Such actions are not the existential actions of free men. They are the actions of men who wish to offend society, but still cringe at the consequence. A man is personally free when he embraces all choices fully and honestly and welcomes all that they bring to his life, be it good or ill.

Societal freedom is the exercise of choice by a group through the operations of free institutions. A group of people achieve self-governance by the establishment of institutions which effectuate their collective wills. From time to time institutions erected for this purpose lose contact with the collective will and become instrumentalities of a few who convert them to their own ends. When this occurs a free people revolt. There is unrest, dissension, and ultimately defiance of order. Those who have exercised personal freedom in a revolt against oppressive institutions stand recognized in history as heroes of man.

Societal freedom in America is manifested by a configuration of free institutions designed to allow a maximum of personal freedom with a minimum of personal consequence. These institutions are the offspring of a revolution inspired by the idea of Freedom. Americans achieve societal freedom through the operation of free institutions. These institutions are all that stand in the way of tyranny. They are all that prevent a return to a social order which fills every unservile choice of man with punitive consequences. Americans want none of this.

Accordingly, we must make a sharp distinction between clear minded free men who revolt against the moribund bureaucracy of an institution which originally was established to implement the collective will, and the aspiring tyrant's efforts to cripple or capture those institutions in behalf of ideologies which are alien to the idea of societal freedom.[3] Such efforts are not intended to accomplish the

---

[3] By *societal freedom* is meant the true *Dasien,* Heidegger's term for the free comradeship of autonomous individuals.

immediate destruction of these institutions. Those involved know full well this cannot be done. The effort is to embarrass institutions, then erode public confidence in them, and finally to parody Freedom itself by conducting a low burlesque. Actually, free institutions can become moribund, and those which do are most susceptible to the burlesque. It is not too much to say that some such institutions, obsessed with administration, are conducting a burlesque of their own.

One can see the low burlesque of Freedom in full form when protestors place their bodies in the doorways of post offices, government buildings, university classrooms, and other institutions consecrated to the preservation of a free society. What does this say except the idea of Freedom is a sham, a fake, something to be mocked? When a gathering of students, ostensibly met for discussion of an issue, refuse by various forms of misconduct to allow speakers to be heard, they burlesque Freedom. When men come to a meeting, then walk out when the main speaker rises, they burlesque Freedom. Their action is a *de facto* denial of Freedom to others and directed to the frustration and embarrassment of the institutions established to achieve the ideal Freedom which has been the object of western civilization for nearly a thousand years.

No one deals sensibly with this kind of problem by invoking massive police power. As a temporary solution police suppression must on occasion be applied. The solution, if there is one, lies, in part, in better teaching of the ideal and, in part, in reforming some free institutions which have become all too far removed from being vital expressions of the societal will. Alas, many institutions have become so impersonal, systematic, and self-serving, they have lost the ideal which brought them into being. In this way they have set the stage for the burlesque. When uncontrollable disorder occurs we should regard it gratefully as the symptom of a serious, potentially fatal malady in the way that a man should appreciate the chill which notifies him to prepare for a serious illness. Whether institutions or men, those who ignore symptoms can be taken suddenly and needlessly.

There are enough corrupt women around to make the low burlesque of Womanhood a plausible reality. There are likewise enough corrupt institutions around to make the low burlesque of Freedom a plausible reality. A society experiences beauty when it realizes the ideal of Womanhood. A society experiences the vitality of free institutions when it realizes the ideal of Freedom. The ubiquitous presence of the low burlesques of both Women and Freedom demonstrates the incapacity of our people to abstract these principles with sufficient force and clarity to appreciate them fully. Western men of the white race have known freedom only briefly. American negroes have yet to know it. The hope is that it will not be lost before all come to know it.

ABSTRACT NOUNS AND SYMBOLS. How does one teach the abstract noun? Womanhood and Freedom are both abstract nouns, and they stand largely untaught. The most critical words in language are abstract nouns. There are many of them. How are they taught? A good beginning can be made in that rich and varied lore called children's literature. There is a charming little story called "The Little Red Hen." What is the story about? Virtually every child knows it is about animals which talk with each other. It rounds, rolls, and repeats in that singsong style in which children delight. But the story is about justice. Those who will work shall eat; those who will not shall not eat. Justice is an abstract noun. It is one which men spend their lives trying to learn. Great institutions are consecrated to the search for it. It has been called the end of order. Children seek it even before they arrive in school. They take turns, share, mete out punishments, and make rules. Everyone has heard the child voice cry: "No fair!" Children's literature is pervaded by abstract nouns. The task of teaching is to develop these nouns into meaningful ideals. Good teachers have always done this; they are doing it now. But, unfortunately, many, perhaps most, classroom teachers pass by the challenge to abstract the principle or the ideal from the noun. They are satisfied, too satisfied, when a child finds the printed word intelligible by the general cognate standards of reading achievement.

Children's thought is capable of abstraction. If nothing else, modern mathematics has demonstrated this. Nothing in education has a greater influence over what children are becoming as humans than the feelings they develop toward the abstract nouns and symbols which represent the qualitative forces in life. What are other such nouns? Courage, Loyalty, and Integrity are examples of personal ideals. Friendship, Leadership, and Fellowship represent interpersonal ideals. Musicianship, Craftsmanship, Seamanship, Salesmanship, and Statesmanship are a few of the many kinds of work ideals. Any listing must also include the more remote metaphysical values such as Truth, Knowledge, Piety, and Faith. Now what do we have to say about these things to our young people?

It seems that to each generation we say less and less. Although we have no difficulty in admitting that abstract nouns stand directly as the *qualitative* aspects of life and although the literature of the modern profession of education adds up to one long exhortation for *quality*, the abstract nouns are largely ignored. What is the reason? There is now in our schools and colleges an obsession for cognate achievement. This is the kind of achievement one measures on tests. In essence it is the knowledge of "being in itself." It is the objective knowing which man does. This means he is an object which knows other objects. But this is the trivial knowledge of his life. It is not the knowledge which leads to choice.

For example, there was once a man with a love of Privacy. (Privacy is one of the great metaphysical rights). He lived in a suburban neighborhood, so when he walked in the back of his house he was keenly aware that his movements were open to the scrutiny of others. Whether they actually were is not so important as the feeling they could be. So he allowed his privet hedge to grow, and grow it did. Soon it rose to a height of 20 feet, and he derived great satisfaction from the secluded nature of his retreat. However, neighbors did not share his delight in the hedge. But it was, after all, his. One day he sold the house and moved away. The first thing the new owner did was get a tractor and pull all those mammoth privet hedges out root by root.

This example demonstrates the knowledge of decision or choice. It is possible that by their test scores the two men would reveal their knowledge of privet hedges to be similar and nearly equal. But how do they feel about the hedge? To one it was a beautiful bastion, both symbol and instrument to his ideal of Privacy, and to the other it was a hideous obstacle to his view of his neighbors. We do not make such choices only on the basis of what we know. More often we make these choices on the basis of what we feel.

The knowledge of object (being in itself) is called cognate. The knowledge of feeling (being for itself) has been called affective. It is the affective knowledge which is neglected in today's curriculum. The most obvious reason for this is that it can't be measured. Even though cognate knowledge is inferior knowledge in the sense that it is not so decisive in human action, the stress put upon it grows with each year. Prior to the modern era of achievement testing (testing of cognate knowledge) schools were not so squeamish about facing up to values. The renowned McGuffey Reader made no bones about its intention to instill certain ideals in those who were learning to read. But the students who learned to read by McGuffey were not measured on cognate grade level achievement standards. Reading achievement tests came later.

It is matter of wide agreement that one's knowledge of how to work is less critical than how one *feels* about work to the ultimate success or failure of the worker. Similarly, it is widely agreed that the most careful and critical students of American history are not the most devoted citizens. How does one feel about being an American? How does one perceive the idea of America, and how does he feel about the idea? If we fail in transmitting the strength and vitality of our civilization to oncoming generations, the failure will come as a consequence of the unwillingness of democracy to ordain that education enter the domain of values in a direct way. The abstract nouns and symbols are not just words and pictures; they are ideas. When they are deeply felt or *valued,* their burlesque is not permitted.

CRISIS OF VALUES. It is recognized that any social arrangement worthy of the name of civilization is always in something of a crisis of values. The crisis is usually expressed in the abrasive relationships between older and younger generations. Our pagan and biblical literature frequently reflects a perennial anxiety about the attitudes of the youth. More than one scholar has supposed that the Athenian jury which martyred Socrates was afflicted in part by despair over the excesses of young men whose rebellious propensities were seemingly stimulated by the great sage. Conflict over values is certainly not new, but this does not reduce the contemporary problem. There is good reason to think the concerns of today are unique and more difficult than men have faced in the past.

One reason for this is in the fact that man's capacity for self-destruction is now absolute. The bridges back to barbarism have burned away; we could never make it back alive. Another reason is uncertainty on the part of the adult generation as to what our values are. It is fairly clear what they were, but there is doubt about what they are and confusion about what they are becoming. This is because we accept change as a master of process rather than idea.

The philosophy of today is a philosophy of process. We look to means—hoping, thinking that means alone will discover ends. Advances in technology and medicine tend to foster this obsession with process until serious thought about the values and ends of our civilized order is found to be not even academically respectable. For this reason processes tend to become an end. Better management of procedures becomes a standard. It matters not so much where we are running just so we are running well and faster. It is small wonder, therefore, that we cannot speak to our children with coherent language about matters of worth. This makes the modern crisis of values unique and more difficult. How can the young respect a generation so unsure of itself?

We cannot mount a curriculum for children which alleges to focus on needs and problems without citing the standards and values which make a need a need or a problem a problem. For three decades or more we have regarded school dropouts as a problem. Perhaps it is. But why is it a problem? Is schooling an end in itself? What is the value involved? Public journals are full of complaints about presumed immorality among certain teen-age groups, but there are very few philosophically defensible arguments presented to teen-agers or anyone else on why the morals which they so capriciously set aside are worth credence. Why, in an age when disease and pregnancy can be easily avoided, should sexual promiscuity not flourish? Adults will say to themselves and to each other that it should not, but what rationale do they offer to a young mind trained to respond to the authority of its own reason and to that alone? Alas, they have little to say except to appeal to sentiment; this does not go far.

Socrates, on the other hand, knew how to convince young men that there were true ideas that could serve as the basis for happiness. However, professional philosophy today does not examine ideas. This work has fallen to behavioral scientists who look at processes. A few of these go so far as to suggest that if we know enough about how things work we will thereby understand what they are and what they should do. They avoid questions of *matter* and *mind* and deal only with a flow of things.

How long have we looked upon reading as merely a process children learn? The goals of a school reading program are formed by those anonymous persons who write or select the items for standardized tests. We may have done a terrible thing. We have raised up four or five generations with a capacity to read philosophy but with a distinct preference for pornography. In reality, for a great many, we have opened one more way for them to debase their lives. Yet we go on thinking that reading is a process. Teachers are trained to teach reading with a zeal for making the printed word intelligible— that and nothing more. So children, not developed to perceive beauty in word, resort to the traumas of the low literature because out of the low literature they get *feeling*. The animal shocks of sex, gambling, and violence give hue, color, and texture to the drab moments of life. There is so much more in the word which could enrich their lives, but children are not educated to receive it. We may have done a terrible thing, indeed.

The humane teacher, therefore, seeks to bring the learner to higher levels of abstraction in regard to both noun and symbol. More than this, the teacher encourages the child to have sentiment about these things. Here is where this thesis undergoes attack. What are the "right" sentiments regarding Womanhood, Manhood, Parenthood, or the ideals of craft such as Musicianship, Statesmanship, or Workmanship? Critics will say our obligation to objectivity forbids that we deliver the learner to personal leanings in respect to those ideals. But this is nonsense—sheer nonsense. Any civilization which is even moderately serious about its own continuance will not allow its greatness to be devalued by each new generation in the pious expectation that the young in two short semesters of childhood and adolescence will generate the sentiments that have been building in western man for over 2,000 years. There is much greatness in western man, and the key to understanding it is through the abstract nouns and symbols by which it is represented. Thus, the humane teacher cannot stop when his students "recognize" words and "comprehend" stories. He must acquaint children with the greatness inherent in their civilization.

The power of literature must become power in the reader. His relationships to people and to things are cultivated, honed, and heated. He is brought to enter upon fuller, more ample levels of being; and he enters into communication with a family of great men extended vertically in time who have shared the same ideals, sensed their beauty, and rejoiced at the capacity they held in helping man transcend the material life. He enters his home library for instant communication with Plato, Aristotle, Augustine, Aquinas, Milton, and countless others, who stand as every educated man's personal consultant on manhood.

When we moved from the old schoolhouse into the new building we forgot something. Like the ancient picture of the second cousin twice removed, it was left hanging there when we moved to our new address. Someday someone should drive by the old place and pick it up. What is it? It is the abstract noun. Abstract nouns are the blocks out of which children build values. But they are more than blocks; they are cubes full of feeling. If we are to come anywhere near resolving our unique and difficult crisis of values, these familiar words will help us become as men and women while we maintain our concern with what they can do as workers in factory, field, and commerce.

This is not a voice of despair. There is darkness, but the sun is rising. In one of his essays Cassius Keyser told of a philosopher who once asked, "Where is the sun?" One of his students pointed and replied, "Off yonder in the heavens."[4] But the sage replied, "You are right and you are not right; the sun is also wherever it shines." The task before American education is to teach every child to perform the feats of abstraction necessary for the development of a coherent value syntax. It has never been done before on the scale contemplated by this goal. However, never before was it so desperately needed. Humane teachers have always done it. They are doing it now. The light of humane teaching shines wherever there is a teacher with the vision, commitment, and art to deal with human beings who are in a state of *becoming*. There are many such teachers now, and more on the way. Soon the light will spread to other places where now there is only the darkness of raw, measured academic achievement.

------

[4] Cassius J. Keyser, *The Human Worth of Rigorous Thinking* (New York: Scripta Mathematica, Yeshiva College, 1940), p. 198.

Part II

THE ANATOMY OF RELIGIOUS VALUES

Blessed Assurance

I have a dog—
   he's just a plain dog.
But he doesn't know it;
   his tail is up; his head is high
   as if he were mayor of the town.
He doesn't know
   he's just a dog.

You can't tell him—
   he can't be shown
He's just a baseless pup,
   runt of a nondescript litter,
   mother undistinguished, father
unknown.
He's an unplanned harvest
   of caprice.

His baronial strut,
   his lordly manner
Unfit a cur so ignoble,
   but there is no way to reach him
   and teach him of his disgrace.
Even if I could,
   I wouldn't.

Prefatory Remarks:
Happiness and Practical Reason

Heine recounts with great charm an encounter between Immanuel Kant and Lampe, Kant's faithful servant. The old man was said to weep when he understood that Kant's first great critique, that of pure reason, was thought to demonstrate that God has no existence apart from the mind of man. Then, according to Heine, "Immanuel Kant relents and shows that he is not merely a great philosopher but also a good man, and half good naturedly, half-ironically he says: 'Old Lampe must have a God, otherwise he can never be happy. Now a man ought to be happy in this world; practical reason says so; Well—I am quite willing that practical reason should also guarantee the existence of God.'"[1]

The tale may be apocryphal, but it is relevant. The valuing of the human mind, that which orders the inner world, functions on beliefs. The interiors of all values are religious beliefs. In many cases these beliefs are rooted in theism. But theistic beliefs are not the only religious possibilities. There are many others. The God which lived for old Lampe was as real for Lampe as anything could be real. However, there are many other gods which people accept into belief. These, too, are real. The practical reason[2] simply asserts that at the deep base of every man is a moral force. Traditional religions would imply that this force is God. Much of mankind has found believing this a great happiness. *Perhaps this is the strongest argument for the existence of God.*

Some choose other alternatives, and this is their existential right. However, theistic alternatives are no longer given adequate exposure in the education of American children. This is a moral offense against the individual. Moreover, there are indications of deterioration in the quality of religious experience in America. It is necessary to ask, therefore, if this deterioration is associated in any way with the decline of theism in American life. Is America, like old Lampe, weeping because God "has succumbed."

---

[1] Heinrich Heine, *Religion and Philosophy in Germany*, Trans. John Snodgrass (London, Keagan, Paul, French, Trubner, & Co., Ltd., 1891.), p. 119.
[2] The categorical imperative.

The little dog described on the introductory page is a proud and happy animal. There is no known reason for either the pride or the happiness. Indeed, this dog should not only weep but also hide himself in shame. He doesn't, and there is no way to make him understand that he should. This dog will go on feeling good about himself, and nothing can be done to set the matter right. This is blessed irony, for on the scale of cosmic values (if such exists) this happy little dog may very well be right about himself. Similarly, it might be a very good thing if atheists would learn to leave others alone.

The three essays in Part II deal with the quality of religious experience, the problem of religious alternatives, and the struggle of the mind to formulate religious values.

ON RELIGIOUS EXPERIENCE

(The American Catharsis and the Role of Loyalty in Emendating Religious Experience)

TYRANNY IN THE STREETS. Democracy usually butchers its heroes. Whatever gift is created for the common man, be it inspiration, idea, law, or knowledge, the giver is promptly destroyed. The greater the gift, it seems the swifter and surer the destruction. Socrates gave western knowledge a critical spirit; the Athenian democrats gave him poison. Mindful of this, Aristotle departed the same city in haste wishing, as reputedly he said, to prevent the city from "sinning twice against philosophy." Jesus Christ offered western man an inspired life. The mob demanded and was given his death. Eighteenth century Parisians tolerated a licentious monarch and then beheaded a king who adored simple virtues. Poor Tom Paine—the zealots of our young republic never forgave his brilliance. Jefferson showed him courtesy, as well he might, for even then storms of vilification were blowing in upon his beloved Monticello. No American president was more abused than Lincoln. Woodrow Wilson died dispirited, still clinging grimly to the ideal of global order. Herbert Hoover, humanitarian, conservationist, was bathed in abuse for the second half of his life. The greater the American president, the more brutal is his derogation. In recent days we have seen even more of this. The crowd seems to say, "Do me a favor, then I will kill you; but in years to come your gift will be praised, and we will teach our children and their children of your greatness."

It is the catharsis. Our Teutonic, Frankish, Semitic, African, Indian, and Etruscan forebears all knew and experienced the abominations of human sacrifice. It was a religious experience. It cleansed them. The precious was laid upon the altar and stabbed, thus filling the beholders with pity, awe, remorse, and fear. And they departed those bloody and smoking scenes pensive, solemn, stricken, but more humane. Lamentation and grief purge the animal juices and bring men to the ideal of manhood. Aristotle in his well known *Poetics I* proclaimed tragedy to be the highest and first among the dramatic arts. Its function is to cleanse. Someone admirable falls into misfortune, usually by his own doing, and as fate weaves its ironies the audience openly wails in remorse, and they depart, each cleansed of impurities.

Did public hangings deter crime? No, but the value is not in deterring a potential felon; it is the common man who is thus moved to suspiration and awe. He feels a strange empathy with the dangling figure. The mob which lynches ceases to be a mob when the rope draws tight. They come to their infamy as one, but as each departs, he is alone with his shame and guilt. For a while, at least, the ugliness is out of him. But it grows again as the days, weeks, and months go by. Then, once again, he needs the catharsis.

No present American can forget those emotion-racked days which followed the assassination of a young president. Hour after hour the melancholy scenes were recreated by television. America, eyes brimming, tried to give sorrow words, failed, and sat utterly stunned by grief and self-doubt. Those poignant weeks of mourning were then followed by miracles of constructive social action. Pundits and prophecy makers still record astonishment at the surge of national unity, purpose, and policy which followed. America had a catharsis. Those previously venomous in denouncing the fallen leader could not recall the day that he was not deeply appreciated and revered. Some who voted *against* him could not recall how they had marked the ballot.

But time passed and the ever-flowing juices of animality started once again to fill the iniquitous reservoirs which seem ever-filling in the human psyche. Again, the derogations began to mount. Incoherent polemics, insulting caricatures filled the air and marred the pages, and a president who had tried hard and done much gave to the mob his political life. Then they cheered, thanked him, and began to honor him as never before. A great civil rights leader and a young senator, both in the fullness of their promise, died of assassins' bullets, and proposed laws which had lain dormant in committees came alive and were passed. Again, the people are having their catharsis. Suddenly, again, they are better people. They discovered the good.

THE LOST CHILDREN OF THE ALLEGHENIES. Examples of

this kind simply illustrate the human catharsis at a level of national experience. On a smaller scale, American communities, families, and private citizens experience expurgations on a smaller but no less meaningful scale. A community disaster will immediately result in spontaneous humanitarian enterprise. On the occasion of death, a family feud may cease for a while. The perturbation and sadness of a man who must put to sleep a loving and loyal dog will make him, for a time, more gentle with all the rest of the world.

Midway through the nineteenth century a hunter from a small frontier village some twenty miles from Johnstown, Pennsylvania, entered the woods. Unknown to him, his two small children, a boy and a girl, followed. Hours later when he returned to the settlement the children were not to be found. Soon a realization that the children were lost began to spread; the word went out, and search parties were organized. From the town of Johnstown came wagonloads of men of all ages. It was dead winter then, and the boreal perils of mountain winds were well known to those who roam upon the slopes of the Alleghenies. Yet, for four bitter days and nights the searchers, almost hand in hand, combed the hills and valleys. Hundreds of men, women, and boys left hearth, home, and responsibility. Storm, frostbite, and piercing discomfort only seemed to strengthen their resolution. Finally, the inexorable truths of nature chilled even the last hope; the children were not found. Weeks later, a legend holds, a distant relative had a dream which, upon his awakening, led him to their location. The two were found frozen, huddled together in each other's arms. Now a marker stands on the spot which commemorates the "Lost Children of the Alleghenies."

The marker is to the memory of two children, but it stands also as a reminder of how beautiful a man can be when he is purged by his own emotions. This was not just one man; there were hundreds of beautiful men. For many of them, those moments near the Blue Knob Summit and across the Laurel Highlands were their "finest hours." These became their days of high favor in the sight of mankind. The monument, if anything, is to what a man can be but only occasionally is, or to what a man can do but only occasionally does. Scratch a man and you will find humanity; but scratch deeply—hurt him. The monument to the children is deep in the woods, only occasionally seen. Perhaps this is as it should be.

TOWARD A CIVILIZED RELIGIOUS EXPERIENCE. Unlike our

primitive forebears, we do not advocate or openly want human sacrifice. Even animal sacrifice is considered heinous. Despite our posture on religious freedom, we would outlaw any religion which offered such things as part of its ritual. But despite this, we cannot say that man's need for the catharsis and the means he uses to achieve it is really any different from the dim and unremembered past of our primitive religions. Reason has ruled that we shall not set out to create suffering through institutions of religion and government, but our nature seems to continue demanding it. The public press and broadcast which are governed by consumer response select for exposure to the public those events which produce the strongest response. These same selected events are further dramatized by journalistic styles which deliberately inflame human imagination. In this way, grotesque fantasies are manufactured to nourish the ire in man's spirit. As popular irritation grows into a tide of paranoidal feeling, reactionary incidents generate the raw material for even greater fantasies. As the agitation of mind and spirit compounds and mounts, rationality departs—until the catharsis occurs; then men once again become men.

The civilized religious experience is one factor which brings relative stability to this hopeless cycle. As indicated above, the primitive religions used human and later animal sacrifice to produce the sense of holiness. The recognized modern religions do not. Christianity does have as a central aspect the rites of the last supper. To some Christians the celebration is allegorical, to others it is real. In a sense this is as close as modern religions come to the experience of sacrifice. The literal Christian whose belief is at the level of religious commitment does encounter a *sense of holiness* in the communion or the mass. It is further actualized by confession. This, then, is his cleansing, and because he partakes of it regularly it helps him to remain securely and stably within the bounds of reason and rational action.

The Judaic and Islamic religions accomplish the same effect in different ways. That is to say, they, too, achieve catharsis by actualizing or elevating the sense of the holy. Ritual, sincerely entered and performed, can have these felicitous results. However, it all rests upon belief. A man, to derive human benefits from his religion, *must believe the decisive events which are sustained by his religious tradition.* Specifically, a Christian must believe that Christ willingly went upon the cross to redeem the world. This is both central and paramount.

Believing in Jesus' virgin birth and resurrection is central to certain Christian groups, but not to all. However, the idea of Jesus' sacrifice for redemption is central to all. To Jews the idea that Moses was sent by God to lead the Israelites from Egypt is central. To Moslems, the idea that Mohammed received from the hands of God an unfinished version of the Koran, is central. The key to a religious experience is that Christians, Jews, and Moslems, *believe* the central and decisive event in their religious tradition occurred and that it occurred for a supernatural purpose.

If we can stand apart from the modern western religions and compare them with the primitive religions, we gain at least one measure of the distance man has traveled from primitive life to modern civilization. Instead of achieving a sense of the holy by human or animal sacrifice, self-mutilation, or magic, modern religions achieve a sense of the holy by faith in holy events and the systems of ideas which are associated with those events. It is clear that modern and primitive religions have in common the regularity of ritual and dogma, and both produce the purifying effects. But modern religions treat man as something more than a creature who simply believes in being alive and is only moved to awe and wonder when confronted by death or suffering, and this is the critical distinction between the modern and the primitive. The modern religions flourish in man's capacity to idealize and order, to will and reason from a foundation of belief and reverence.

What is the melancholy meaning of the fact that the humane in American life rises to dominance only when a sacrifice or tragedy occurs? The meaning is all too clear. Sacrifice or tragedy is the only kind of religious experience which seems to include all major sectors of the public. As such, it offers testimony to the general inadequacy of the routine religious experience in American life; and it stands as a discouraging indication of the small distance which separates modern and primitive man on the scale of civilized values. Only by tragedy or sacrifice do we move upward, but the gain in any event is only for a time. The mass, unmoved by a recognized and regular religious experience, will soon be back to vilification and violence until it gets its tragedy and catharsis.

SOCIAL GODS: LIFE, WEALTH, POWER: It would be an error to say that this suggests that the American people are not religious. They are deeply religious; indeed, all men are religious. The question is:

How are the American people religious? In what do they believe at the deep base of existence? What do they accept as decisive in their lives? They believe in being alive. They believe in having things. They believe in having political rights. They believe in some form of social justice. They have certain loyalties to selected institutional forms and symbols. There are a great many beliefs which characterize the American people. All of these beliefs are aspects of their religious nature. A deeper analysis would show that aside from the basic belief in life itself nearly all other American beliefs are social or cultural in origin. Perhaps even the *life theory* of the American people is social. America apparently values by consensus. Somehow these values, these predispositions, rise out of the ferment and turbulence of American life, and they take form in social consensus. In this kind of *milieu,* consensus stands in the place where a God stands in a more orthodox theologic structure. America is moved religiously when its consensual values are struck down by misfortune or malfeasance.

It is neither surprising nor unusual to find that citizens of a democracy have made democracy its own absolute. This has happened before. The central question is whether or not in all democracy such a result is necessary or inevitable. Certainly there are institutions within a democracy which articulate values which are independent of social consensus and by their own enterprise tend to elevate the consensus. But the vitality of these religions and educational enterprises in America has been sapped and increasingly suppressed by the law givers and judges who require elimination of the functions by which values which are independent of consensus are fostered and engendered. In Amercian education, if one seeks to teach values, he must be certain to convince the public that he is doing anything but teaching values. It seems American jurisprudence has discovered that children have a right to grow to maturity without encountering in organized education anyone who has a value of any kind except the sovereign values in America; the beliefs in life, wealth, and power. This is how America is coming to be religious, and it is not a prospect which pleases.

The prospect does not please because it is not the idea of America which we all have come to love; but the universal adoration of life, wealth, and power is, alas, becoming the unfortunate reality of what is called the American experience in democracy. This makes us understand that regardless of material abundance, the quality of American life will continue to degenerate unless the institutions of education and religion succeed in implanting other values and unless these same institutions succeed in laying the grounds for a superior form of religious experience, one which does not depend only upon the witnessing of the tragic loss of life, wealth, or power by a figure so familiar that the bereavement touches and moves us all. We simply must do better in religious education. America, as we know it, has no alternative path upward, and the downward path makes sense to no one.

Wherein lies hope? If we have hope, then it is within us. If hope is not in us, then it is nowhere. Whereof lies wisdom? Wisdom is always close at hand. but the kind of wisdom of which we speak must be embraced by America; we cannot merely stare at it cynically, or inspect it academically, and expect it to become part of us. We must warm to it and embrace it. If universities remain aloof to it, then we must have new universities. If churches remain cold to it, we must have new churches. Wisdom is close at hand, and our institutions must help us embrace it, or we must have new institutions.

THE VALUE OF CONVENTIONAL WISDOM. We owe much of our wisdom and also much of our cynicism to Socrates. Perhaps even Socrates would say to us that men now are much too cynical and the wisdom in our heritage is undervalued. Once he undertook to examine Euthyphro, a young man apparently intent upon killing his father. This youth came to the city to prosecute his father for murder. Euthyphro, it seems, was certain of the values of the gods. One would not expect Socrates to remain aloof from such a fascinating confrontation, and he did not. By his customary questions he demonstrated that Euthyphro did not have sufficient knowledge of the gods or of anything else to justify scorn of a relationship in which his civilization had discovered great wisdom.

The youth of all time, strong in the certainties they feel, are ever tempted to commit the crime of parricide. Young teachers have always encouraged youth to depart from the wisdom which as children they embraced, for young teachers. too, are enthralled by certainties they feel, and so they often teach that conventional wisdom deserves contempt, but conventional wisdom was long in convening. The bright new knowledge of modern men, like that of Euthyphro, is not sufficient to justify the scorn of conventional wisdom.

Conventional wisdom holds that a man must be a believer and not a doubter. He must be loyal, not uncommitted. In his brilliant study of the *Philosophy of Loyalty*, Josiah Royce indicates that loyalty is good for the loyal man. A man chooses that to which he devotes himself. The cause which a loyal man elects, he then embraces by virtue of the "assent of his own will." A loyal man has a cause, and the cause is important to him; it rises above his creature needs and beautifies him. Devotion ennobles a man.

However, a cause may not be just; it may not be a good cause. Royce goes on to point out that one man's loyalty is just or good only to the extent to which it does not destroy another's loyalties. What can this mean? Loyalty to one's race is good, but if that loyalty is of such a nature that it by its exercise destroys another man of another race and, thereby, the loyalties the other holds for his race, then the cause of the destroyer (loyalty to his race) is bad. A man can know if the cause to which he is loyal is a good one by asking: "By my active devotion to this cause am I destroying another man or destroying his cause?" Thus, Royce enjoins us to be loyal to loyalty. This formulation is a specific application of the Kantian imperative, "Act so that the maxim of your will shall always hold good as a universal legislation." Conventional wisdom is, therefore, sustained by that tradition of philosophy which moves always in the direction of first principles.

A man's belief must not, therefore, be harmful to a belief to which others are loyal. The militant atheist is not, by this analysis, possessed of a good cause. If in his loyalty to atheism he acts so as to turn the climate of public life entirely congenial to atheism, then he acts to destroy the loyalties others hold to theism. Why is this so? It is so because the ideas of theism and atheism are antithetical. An environment which eliminates one must of necessity disfavor the one which is eliminated. Only a public environment which is congenial to both would offer men the full freedom of choice.

But this is not what American jurisprudence has produced. Nurturing an illusion that neutrality is the thing, the courts have laid foundations which are distinctly favorable to the atheistic alternative. In a neutral environment, atheism is exposed but theism is not. Because this is destructive of theistic loyalties, the court decisions of the recent decade are, on the grounds of the categorical imperative, immoral.

THE NEGLECT OF LOYALTY. This state of affairs, though recent, has been long in coming. Royce, writing near the turn of the century, warned of the low state of American moral education. He declared that we as a nation have been "forgetting Loyalty,"[1] and we have not been cultivating loyalty in our institutional order. Loyalty is something every human is made to possess. However, he does not possess it by virtue of life alone. He must be prepared in such a way as to want to give himself to something. But giving of oneself is not cultivated in the contemporary social order where belief is in life, wealth, and power. None of these things imply giving; but rather they imply acquiring. None of these things establish a propensity to be loyal to anything but that which gives life, wealth, or power; and alas, loyalty in such cases is not to a thing itself but is in the interests of what that thing can return. Loyalty is not regarded as its own reward. Few have not heard the poignant complaint, "I gave my life to *the company* and all I have to show for it is a gold watch." It is true that a man does not give his life for a gold watch. Properly understood, devotion or loyalty to a thing brings *meaning* to life. The "gold watch," therefore, symbolizes that during many years of devoted service, his life held an added dimension of meaning. Loyalty in this case is its own reward.

If those things to which a man is giving his life were suddenly removed, his life would just as suddenly become absurd. It would not again be meaningful until he found other things to which he could be loyal. It is the failure of our educational institutions to cultivate the propensity for loyalty which causes so many Americans to feel the meaninglessness and absurdity in their lives. Such men are often then driven into the arms of the Freudian professions, there to be counseled that the imperfections of man are inevitable and assured that among these imperfections rests the cause of their distress. This, alas, they often believe and, thereby, become loyal to their own imperfections. It is clear that many Americans are devoted to modes of backsliding.

LOYALTY, BELIEF, AND RELIGIOUS EXPERIENCE. Thus far it has been asserted that loyalty to a chosen cause or belief is good in a man and that there is a way of knowing which are and which are not moral causes or beliefs. It has also been asserted that there is and has been a neglect of the idea of loyalty in American education. All humans are imbued with a capacity for loyalty. This capacity should be (but is not now) consciously developed by American religion and educational institutions. Finally, it has been asserted that loyalty to a

---

[1] Josiah Royce, *The Philosophy of Loyalty* (New York: The Macmillan Co., 1908), pp. 14-21.

cause or belief brings meaning to life. Absence of a belief or cause produces meaninglessness or absurdity in life. All of this is consistent with both conventional wisdom and philosophies which move under the direction of first (or *a priori*) principles.

Now it is asserted that strong loyalty to cause or belief makes possible a significant and regular religious experience. What does a man believe? And is he loyal to his belief? If a man holds a belief which is, according to the above-stated moral criterion, a good belief, and if he is loyal to that belief, then regular religious experience is possible and the man will be stable, rational, and strong. He will not require a massive catharsis by way of public tragedy or sacrifice for cleansing. His purification is obtained from the clarity which comes from ordering the events and circumstances of his life upon the beliefs which he (in this sense) *enjoys*.

A Christian with a heightened propensity for loyalty can turn to that belief which is decisive and holy for Christians and *enjoy* a religious experience. But, again, what is the belief that is decisive and holy to Christians? It is not simply a belief in the institutions, the laws, or the men who comprise Christendom. The real center, the real law, the real institution of Christian fellowship is a living personality, the incarnate Son of God, the risen Lord, Who was revealed by His life and work among men, and Whose presence is manifested by a Holy Spirit. The authentic Christian believes in the Word made flesh, in *Christ Himself*. This is the uniqueness of Christianity and, therefore, the uniqueness of Christians. For any Christian who holds to this belief, any communication with Christ, be it called mass or communion, is a significant religious experience. It performs a catharsis.

The Jewish, Moslem, Buddhist, and Brahman religions all have central beliefs which also make significant religious experience possible. Atheism takes many forms; upon analysis, it is clear that atheists can be devout and devoted to a belief. Indeed, many atheists are more devout and devoted than those who profess a loyalty to a recognized theistic religion. Many atheists might be considered as belonging to a *Religion of Good Conscience*. Belief in and loyalty to dictates of good conscience can furnish the basis for a high quality of religious experience. However, this kind of religion demands high levels of rationality, higher by far than many of its celebrants attain. Too many of these, unfortunately, belong to a *Religion of Good Conscience Selectively Applied*. Panentheists who believe that God reveals His will in the social consensus are also capable of a deep religious experience, but this religion also demands high levels of rationality—so high, in fact, that the belief itself is very difficult to understand. Poorly understood, it results in the kind of mob action and the ultimate need of mob catharsis referred to in the introductory paragraphs of this essay. It is possible for a religion based upon a belief that God is shown in the race consciousness and rational like-mindedness of man, but this man must be *governed by reason* and not simply a lust for life, wealth, and power. To such a believer the operation of his reason is a religious experience and a continuing catharsis.

Therefore, the issue of this discourse is not the inherent rightness or wrongness of any of the modern religions. All of modern religions have central events or ideas which are believable; and manifestly, all have the capability of providing significant religious experience. The issue is whether the American people are or are not *sufficiently loyal* to the central beliefs of their religions for their respective religious experiences to be *significant* rather than *perfunctory*. Too much of the church and synagogue life in America is perfunctory. Too much of the church and synagogue life is devoted to extra-religious concerns. This is so obviously and generally recognized that the judgment that Americans are not *sufficiently loyal* to the central beliefs of their religions appears *highly tenable*.

THE LEARNING OF LOYALTY. The religious and academic institutions must, therefore, make more of loyalty. How does one teach loyalty? Loyalty is not taught in the conventional sense. It is better to think of loyalty as being learned. Aristotle suggested that one learns to do by doing. One learns to be loyal by being with loyal people who are in the act of loyalty. Royce suggested that loyalty is, *"the willing and practical and thorough-going devotion of a person to a cause."* Moreover, he suggested that loyalty is expressed in some sustained and practical way. There is an example in the devotion of a craftsman to the ideals of his craft or the devotion of a scholar to the ideals of scholarship or the devotion of a captain to the requirements of seamanship. Similar expressions are in the devotion of players to team, devotion of family to kindred, and devotion of student to school.

Loyalty is learned in small groups and transfers to beliefs which are also learned and held by small groups. Such has been the strategy employed by many revolutionaries who succeeded in developing such devotion to cause that regimes were overthrown which possessed great conventional power but little loyalty. The modern movement called International Communism has employed this historic formula to the consternation of our own republic and its established religions and political institutions. But Christendom should remember that these small groups constituted the same learning arrangements which first spread and fostered Christianity itself, and Judaism should remember that Jews have frequently resorted to small group activity in the preservation of Judaism which has been alternately exiled and oppressed for nearly two thousand years.

Think now of our large schools with several thousands of students who are related to its operations through a computer. They are "punched cards" in a binary number system. Think also of large church organizations with power centralized far from the membership. Large schools and large churches cannot develop loyal propensities in youth unless they design to have them active in small groups. To the chagrin of some academicians and intellectuals this would mean a kind of new emphasis on extra-class activities. However, if those devoted to cognate academic learning are called upon to recollect those experiences that were meaningful in their own personal development, they are often heard to narrate of service to a school newspaper, of preparing scenery and costumes for a school play, of performing second clarinet in the school band, or of playing left guard on the football team. All of these undertakings call for devotion, much of it for the sake of devotion. Do you want a loyal man? Then find one who gave himself to something in school.

EMENDATING THE RELIGIOUS EXPERIENCE. If we wish to improve the quality of religious experience in American life and eliminate the recurrence of mob catharsis, we must embrace and not reject conventional wisdom. This means encouraging loyalty and belief rather than detachment and doubt. An institution, either a school or a church, which seeks to foster loyalty must create an environment in which loyalty is learned. Student activities in this light are not incidental diversions from academic experience but vital educational enterprises in their own right. We must not go on streaming our children through these incredibly faceless and impersonal systems with contrived standards and invented categories which take the place of human interaction and judgment. Our magnificent effort at public education has left us with a plan for elementary education which does not permit us to look at children as children. Instead they are treated and discussed as mechanisms which must acquire skills. This same massive effort has left us with a secondary education which equates the acquisition of cognate knowledge with education itself. Higher and graduate education increasingly wear this same aspect. Student disorders at this higher level frequently involve persons who are desperately seeking something to which they can be loyal. Not finding it in the institutional order, they seek and find it outside of order.

This is not a polemic against schoolmen and churchmen. If anything, the majority of those who now lead our schools and churches recognize the problem all too well. They want reform, but the word has yet to go out with sufficient strength to summon the public to acceptance of reform. If clergymen who lead congregations continue to be judged by the quality of buildings, the size of congregations, or the amounts which gather in collection plates, they cannot be blamed for trying to make a good showing in these things. Likewise a schoolman who runs his system well knows the system rewards slavishness; and, indeed, he also knows it punishes heresies. But, in the fullness of time, the very obvious need for reform will result in a public demand for reform. Schoolmen and churchmen then should proceed with reform rather than submit to or suffer revolution. Reform for the most part remains under the control of reason. Revolution starts that way but reason soon leaves, and in the interval of its absence destruction reigns. Man's capacity for destruction has now grown so great that revolution is no longer a responsible approach to change.

Clearly, therefore, much can be done to improve the quality of regular and frequent religious experiences in America, and it follows that men who have regular and frequent significant religious experiences are more stable, contented, and assured in their lives. They are not confounded by meaninglessness or absurdity. It is not too much to say that they are better men. The conversation of modern times is heavily burdened with prescriptions for the improvement of society. Society, as some think of it, may exist or it may not. There can be no reasoned assurance that improved social processes or systems improve either society or men. But in the mass catharsis, we have seen again and again that in those shining moments when men are better, society is better. Therefore, there can be a reasoned assurance that better men compose a better society. The business before us, then, is the making of better men. The splendid hope of western civilization is in knowing that we have made so many, that we must know how it is done. The wisdom we must embrace is immediately before us.

THE GOD-IDEAS IN AMERICAN SCHOOLS

It is often said that our schools do not teach religion. The public schools, it is often claimed, are God-less. This is not true. The curricula of American public schools is shot full of divine sentiments or religious values, and God-ideas abound throughout. These, however, go unrecognized. Indeed, they are called by other names. The reason the religious nature of these values or sentiments is not recognized is because they are not associated with expressions of churches, synagogues, or other organized religious groups. In the parlance of law and public discussion, only the doctrines of organized religion are considered religious. No matter how devoutly a man believes something, we are unwilling to call his belief religious unless his belief is embraced by a religious organization. This establishmentarian conception of the word "religion" is a cause of great confusion.

Let us suppose for a moment that there was no such thing as a Christian Church. It is hard to imagine western civilization without it, but dream for a moment that there is somewhere a community wherein no one ever heard of Christendom or the Christian Church. Let us suppose also that there are other organized religious groups which sponsor corporate religious exercises and that nearly everyone in the community takes part in these exercises. Some of these might be Taoist, Buddhist, Shintoist, or Moslem. Now one day a young man picks up a book called *The Gospel of John*. As he reads this book he begins to believe what it teaches. Consequently, he begins to modify and finally reconstitute his values. He may or may not alter his participation in the religious exercises recognized by his community. But now he is becoming a Christian. However, the people of his community not knowing of organized Christianity would undoubtedly think the young man merely has an interesting new outlook on life. Many of them might not like it, but because they can't associate it with an establishment which holds to an acceptance of certain holy events, they would not call the young man's view a religious view.

Morever, if there was a law in that community which held that religions could not be taught in public schools, that law would not apply to Christianity because no one calls it a religion. Consequently, this young man, if he was a teacher could teach about the immortal Christ with impunity in such schools. All this remains possible just so long as no one in this community would assert that the young man was teaching a religion.

The point of this is that in American communities those who hold to religious values *not* associated with organized religious bodies are establishing a near monopoly for these values in the schools. While, at the same time, those values contained in religious expressions having acknowledged attachment to a church, synagogue, or mosque are expressly denied a meaningful presence in public school. Hence, the cry is raised that the schools are God-less. They aren't. All kinds of gods are in our schools, and teachers and students are very religious in their beliefs about these gods. It is very possible that Christian, Jewish, and Islamic partisans would prefer a god-less school to what presently exists. But a school that is either God-less or god-less cannot exist because all education deals in values.

Values can be subjected to various modes of analysis. One very simple mode is to think of a value as having two aspects: interior and exterior. The exterior aspect of a value is what we commonly call an attitude. This is the side of a value which a man shows to his fellow men. If we know a man well we are able to say what he is inclined to do or to think about a given idea or thing. We call this predisposition his "attitude." The interior aspect of a value is religion or belief. A belief becomes religious when the holder clings to it and invests his self in it. Somewhere at the deep base of every religious belief is a God-head or God-idea.

An egg, for example, has an exterior and an interior. We have seen enough of both to think of an egg in each of its two aspects. The shell contains, protects, and identifies to our sensibilities the object which we call egg. Even though we cannot see the interior we know it is there. More than this we know that the vital living aspect of the egg is the interior. When an egg is cracked and its contents spread in a frying pan we note that even this has an exterior and interior reality. Metaphorical reasoning of this serves the purpose of illustration, but it cannot be taken too far. The egg in this case helps dramatize two things: the existence of interior and exterior and the relationship of interior and exterior. One does not exist without the other. It is impossible to think of an egg or a value in any other way. The shells of our values are attitudes. The nuclei of our values are our religious beliefs.

Religion is everywhere. Define a man and the definition must include a religion. All men are in some way religious. Think of it this way: a man's intelligence drives him to inquire about his metaphysical name, address, and destination. There is no one who can give him this in a direct and unequivocal way which satisfies all of the terms and issues which a metaphysician can propose. Therefore, he must choose a belief. A man can choose his belief from among a variety of ideas. He may obtain an answer of his own and believe it; he may hear an answer from someone else and believe it; he may believe that no one has the answer; that is, he may believe there is no answer or that anyone who presents one is lying. There is no provision among any of these alternatives for nonbelief, unbelief, or belief in nothing.

There is no neutral ground. Suppose you are walking in your neighborhood and come upon a man beating a dog. This gives you occasion to examine your beliefs. You can believe the man is right, believe he is wrong, or believe that you should hold no opinion either way and therefore avoid forming one. Notice in each case your attitude is formed out of some kind of belief. In each of the three cases a belief is necessary. But notice also that of the three alternatives a belief that a man should have no opinion and stay out of the matter is probably the most difficult of the beliefs to sustain.

Accordingly, the idea of an unbeliever is impossible of reality in man. Whatever else a man is, he is also a believer. This is why man is in some way religious. A nonreligious man is either insane or impossible. Religion is a universal property of all men. There is no man of whom it can be said with certainty, "He is not religious."

We commonly associate religious beliefs with beliefs in God. Many men are religious in this way. A belief in God is their fundamental belief. But other men may not believe in God. Their belief is in other things; it may be in a god, it may be that there is no God, it may be that they should form no opinion about God, or they may believe, as some do, that all beliefs about God must be opposed. These are all other ways of being religious.

Reasoning, as Plato suggested, operates as a divine necessity. There is, by this same necessity, no alternative to accepting the inevitability of belief and of religion in every man. This is why the decisions of the courts respecting the problem of religion and education are philosophically untenable. Such decisions may represent tradition, sentiment, and the logic of precedent. But when thought on the matter moves in the direction of first principles, the establishmentarian position taken by the courts is found to be inadequate. For this reason the present unsatisfactory legal definition of the word "religion" will be short of life. Already the restlessness of the people is beginning to show.

THEISM. The belief most characteristic of the religious posture of the American people is theism. This belief is of a God external to the world, outside of time, who knows the world, knows he is God, and is capable of action upon the world. Now this God-idea is elaborated on in various ways by the various religious organizations. Theological apologetics resort to teleology, revelation, and intuition. Christianity gives God a temporal presence in the mechanics of the Trinity, it also supplies teleology from the logic of hierarchy and the history of revelation.

Regardless of theological variations, any theistic belief is considered religious simply because the vast majority of American religious organizations hold to it. Thus, when one begins to teach a belief in the existence of God, the claim is quickly raised that this is teaching religion. The claim, of course, is valid.

Because teaching theism is so obviously teaching a religion, the judges can invoke the law against it. However, the irony of the matter is that theism is the only category of God-idea which is not permitted in the school. It has been agreed, of course, that courses *about theism* can be taught. But what is the belief which underlies a permission to teach about theism? The judges believe that God must be presented as something someone else believes in. Even if the teacher believes in God his teaching must not be affected in the least by this belief in God. Now the problem here is that the theism which has been strong in the American religious tradition is *heuristic* in nature. That is to say, God is more than an ostensible being or an academic possibility. God is a personal experience; He is an aspect of experience.

The God of the Christians and the Jews does not wear academic robes. He is not an object of detached and critical scholarship, not to the believer, and not to the religious theist. No, this God is not to be taught *about*. Efforts to do so deprive Him of the meaning He holds for those who include the experience of Him as an aspect of human experience. God, it can be said, is welcome in school, but not as God.

Thus, the irony deepens! Not only is He denied access to the school as God, but He is also phenomenalized as an object of academic inquiry for those who come daily to our centers of education in search of meaning and personal relevance. How can this be justified? Its ultimate justification is that Congress cannot establish a religion. Does it follow on the same base that Congress can disestablish a religion and establish other religions in its place? No, it does not follow. But this appears to be happening. This is the kind of irony which emerges when men use man-made law in place of reason in their search for the right and the just.

PANTHEISM. Theism is the name for one category of God-ideas. The word "pantheism" is used to describe another. Ideas of God assigned to this category place the divine *in the world* or the world in *Him*. In a strict interpretation of the word, only those ideas are pantheistic which establish the divine as all of or parts of the world inhabited by men.

As such, pantheism has numerous expressions. One which in modern times is gaining increasing credence is that God is the collective consciousness of man. Although unspoken, this expression is present and of increasing influence in theories of value offered by social philosophers and social scientists who accept group consensus and social mores as a source of value.

There are various ways to develop such a God-idea. One of them is to suggest that men are more than they seem, even to themselves. For example, a man's consciousness extends only to certain points. But Freudian psychologists insist there is a subconsciousness which is within and is a powerful force in the individual personality. Conversely, some philosophers have speculated on the existence of a superconsciousness The field of the superconscious is not worked upon by the individual intelligence as we commonly conceive it and is, therefore, not known of in the usual sense. Theories of the superconscious suggest that something of each man exists out beyond the region of his awareness. Two men, in different rooms, may be empirically unaware of each other, yet each has a superconsciousness which merges in mysterious ways with the other's. One may have a feeling he is not alone or that someone is near. This matter has been referred to by some as extrasensory perception and has been the object of serious study.

It is but a short distance from the superconscious to a theory that God is somehow the universal union of all consciousness. In this sense

God becomes man's valuation of the world. Some philosophers have written eloquently of the compounding of consciousness into a group mind. Certain modern educational philosophers have suggested that a *learned consensus* might serve as a source of value. This consensus *is* a mysterious thing. It seems real, and some men are more adept than others at reading its signals. Some outstanding businessmen and successful educational and political leaders attribute their own eminence to knowing what "the people want." Now one can operate on this basis without declaring that the consensus is God, but if a man operates as if the consensus is God then reason demands that we think of him as a pantheist regardless of what label he hangs upon himself.

The ideologists who head communistic and socialistic nations are very religious about making propaganda. This is a devout conviction that value in the world is established by a kind of vast social mind which makes itself up on the questions which confront all the people of the world. The common phrase "mobilizing world opinion" is simply a commonplace expression of a very recondite God-idea. We must be careful not to imply that because communists believe it the belief is wrong. There are many who are not communists who are equally resolved in this conviction. We see it by their attitudes (the external side of their values) changing when world opinion (the internal or religious side of their values) changes.

Consensus does change. Accordingly, those who treat the consensus as divine must think that God changes. Moreover, men are not above trying to influence the consensus. Men will say world opinion is for this or that, and the syntax of their expression reveals that world opinion is Right. The socialist nations, convinced that world opinion is on the socialist side, have a strong faith in the historical inevitability of world socialism. This is the *ultimate lift.*

Do we teach this kind of valuing, this kind of consensus reverence, this kind of social sovereignty in social studies? You bet we do. It is perhaps the most pervasive God-idea in the American public school curriculum; and of course, we should teach it. It belongs in the curriculum, but we ought to take the wrappers off and explain it the way it is, as an idea of God. If it has no religious implications, then Quakers and Unitarians are not religious. (Some theists will cheerfully agree that they are not!) If one sits in a Quaker service and waits for the merging of consciousness to create a sense of the meeting, he can readily perceive the faith vested in this idea. Many Unitarians convert their service into a modified group discussion which seems to exemplify their faith in what collective man is brought to think.

To many thinking men this is an appealing approach to life on earth. They see this world as the greatest home of man, and they are very devout. They would deny, in many cases, that this devotion to the consensus is devotion to a god. More than a few would simply proclaim themselves agnostics or atheists. In the commonplace non-establishmentarian definition of religion, this would make them non-religious. However, the commonplace definition is philosophically indefensible and so is the nonreligious posture of those who value by consensus.

PANENTHEISM. Pantheism contains numerous variations and some of these call for categorical refinement. Suppose, for example, one accepts the consensus as God-on-Earth, but also ascribes to God an external presence which is outside of time and beyond the world which men sense. This is a combination of the classical form of theism and pantheism. Some students of religion have called this pan(en)-theism. Such categorization is introduced here for illustrative purposes and is not purported a fully reasoned taxonomy of God-ideas. The condition illustrated is that there are many kinds of God-ideas. In the description of these God-ideas the word "God" may or may not be used. The fact that the word God is not used, however, does not reduce religious strength of the idea.

Most panentheistic ideas use the word God freely.[1] Some Christians have God-ideas which fall in this category. Some pragmatists have opined that God is represented in the process of nature and the problem solving processes of man. God may well be out of the world, but He has no meaning apart from the experienceable processes of men. Many pragmatists assert that theological doctrines which rest on bases external to experienceable process add nothing to our real knowledge of value or rules of conduct.

The late Martin Buber seemed to express belief in a God who has a relationship to all things animate and inanimate. Because he is God he galvanizes these relationships, thereby making them real. Imagine your relationship to the chair on which you are sitting. Are you real? Is the chair real? Or is reality the relationship which exists between

---

[1] See the God-ideas of James, Fechner, and Whitehead as quoted in Charles Hartshorne and William Reese, *Philosophers Speak of God* (Chicago: University of Chicago Press, 1953).

you and the chair. Buber seems really to be suggesting that reality is in relationships. Said he, "primary words do not signify things, but they intimate relations." Man (I) senses the eternal (Thou) through his relationships (I-Thou) with every particular thing. The I-Thou denotes relationship. It is a divine interaction continuum in which each particular relationship (I-Thou) links us dynamically to God. We are, therefore, living in God, but at the same time are partners with God in the work of creation.

This is because men are possessed of will. When a man registers his will on the relationship which exists between himself and God he changes the relationship and changes God. Thus men and God are not only joined in creation, but are also joined in creating each other.

Let us imagine a nonviolent demonstration. What is demonstrated? The *will* of the demonstrators is registered upon all of those with whom they relate (I-Thou). So long as the demonstration remains nonviolent, reality may be altered in the direction of the decisive expression of will. Suppose then the demonstration becomes violent. Fear is aroused in those against whom the violence is brought. *Fear* brings something as decisive as *will* into this living and becoming relationship. Positions harden and the relationship becomes characterized by severe sentiments at either end. Thus, in Buber's view of reality there appears to be better practical grounds for nonviolence than for violence as a mode in demonstration of will. We have seen abundant evidence of this in our own times.

This God-idea conforms to none of our traditional ideas. No one teaches it in school *directly*. But have students adopted the practice of registering their will? Have they begun to discuss relationships as primary reality? Are they learning by demonstrations to alter relationships and reality? Have you read the morning papers?

The world is rapidly overtaking the ideas of Martin Buber. Existentialist theologians have been commented on widely. Someday the world will begin overtaking the God-ideas of Fechner, James, and Whitehead. These are recognized as being from philosophical traditions other than existentialism. But their thought about God reveals these same precepts of the imminence of God. One does not need to turn from the course of his life to find God; the reality of God is in human transactions. As Whitehead declared, "The world's nature is a primordial datum for God; and God's nature is a primordial datum for the world." He accepted Fechner's insight that our volitions are God's impulses. But he went on to assert that God influences us and we in turn influence God. There is activity and creativity on both sides.

There is no need further to mine this rich vein of thought except to say that it opens to men vast new possibilities for belief. In time men will come to believe ideas such as this, and new religious ideas will alter human values. Values are represented in human affairs by what men call attitudes. It may be possible, therefore, to institute and foster new attitudes without resorting to religious organizations, and if we remain true to our present unfortunate habits of language, none of this will be called religious.

ATHEISM. Any explanation of ultimate reality which does not depend upon, allow for, or permit a God is properly called atheistic. Nevertheless, it is a religious position. An atheist has a basic belief. This is his religious choice. His atheism is a religious position. If an atheist teaches atheism he is not teaching a nonreligion; he is teaching a religion.

What kind of faith must an atheist have in order to cling to such a position? He must have faith in his own omnipresence! He must *believe* that his senses have not deceived him. He must *believe* that he has seen all there is to see, has heard all that could be heard, and thought all that could be thought. To believe this requires faith of a magnitude equal to that of any established belief in God. An atheist must believe it *so strongly* that he is willing to deny children a full opportunity to examine alternate beliefs in the same place where his own beliefs grow and shine daily—the principal learning environment of American children and youth, the American public school.

Atheism finds a place in the American school through the sciences, most notably biology. Of course, a biologist may be a theist; many of them are. They are aware that the discipline of biology does not explain ultimate things. However, the *a priori* foundations of the discipline do not admit of supernatural explanations, and this is as it should be. Every event in nature is natural and is associated with natural cause. Life is among those events which are natural; its cause is somewhere in nature for men to discover. Now some philosophies of science do not proscribe atheism in these flat terms. Aristotelian theism (the unmoved mover) is still a prominent notion. The difficulty is that none of these issues are usually given to a neophyte biology student. By ducking the metaphysics entirely, teachers and textbook writers leave the atheistic presuppositions to be grasped by inference.

School counselors are often trained to apply counselling techniques which are based upon theories of Freud or Nietzsche. These theories reduce God to a force within personality, created and used by personality in compensation for imbalances or imperfections. Now the divine is never discussed, but the attitude that a devout religious belief is a handy thing the human psyche uses keeps coming through. God, to Nietzsche, is some kind of race neurosis. Philosophy has produced few atheists more militant than he. Out of all of these views emerges a general attitude that a man devout in an orthodox sense is really in some kind of emotional difficulty.

Although it is generally unrealized, a number of the great figures in American and English literature are unconscious apostles of atheism. Shakespeare may have been, as some authorities insist, a Christian and not estranged from his church. However, the pagan flavor of his work is unmistakable, particularly as presented in many secondary schools. Any Christian values or concepts of cosmic order which Shakespeare may have held as a man are undetected in school. Similarly, many high school teachers are ill-equipped to deal abstractly with influences in works such as those of Shelley; thus, these influences work their subtle effects upon the young readers.

There is a great deal more to teaching literature than meets the eye of casual observers. A great work of literature is great in part because of its value content, and it should be pointed out once again that values have interior and exterior aspects. The exterior of any value is recognized as an attitude. One has not completely examined a value by looking upon only its exterior side. The religious subject matter of any literary work is represented by the God-idea of the author. Teachers must be aware of the interior and exterior aspects of value. One does not take one and leave the other alone. When an egg is taken from the basket the interior comes together with the exterior (if not there is a frightful mess). If one develops an attitude he has developed something religious as well.

CONFUSION AND IRONY. The courts have created confusion and irony. Perhaps it is because, as more than one observer has noted, our legal profession and its operations are such that if half of the lawyers in the country are right, then the other half are wrong. The widely held belief that the dialectics of our adversary system will produce truth or something like truth is in itself a kind of rough-hewn religious faith. The courts, in more than a century of finding for and against the religious organizations, have evolved several definitions of religion. As mentioned before, the court definitions have tended to be establishmentarian in nature. In *Torcaso* vs. *Watkins* (1961) it was determined that the term religion included "Buddhism, Taoism, Ethical Culture, Secular Humanism, and others." But in the *Abington* vs. *Schempp* (1963) decision which out-lawed worship as an aspect of public school experience it ruled against only those religions which practice a conventional worship—i.e., prayer. Prayer is a religious methodology associated with theistic religions. Methodologies associated with *Secular Humanism* or *Ethical Culture* may proceed in the school environment with impunity, and they do.

Now, of course, the perfunctory morning prayer offered in most public schools prior to *Schempp* was not in its performance a worship or religious experience. Veterans of years of morning devotions will concede that these exercises came as close to being nonreligious as anything else in the school day. One value of the *Schempp* decision lies in the fact that the religious education problem for American theists is now out in the open. No longer can they rest content in the illusion that these routine exercises constituted a meaningful experience of God. If theism is to survive, such experiences must come into the lives of the young. They have not been there for some time.

The irony lies in the denial of the very religious freedom the court avows to preserve. Modern philosophical discourse uses the term religion in such a way as to render establishmentarian definitions of the term religion untenable. By its failure to discover the distinctions between the methodologies of theistic and nontheistic religions the court has denied the former and encouraged the latter. One cannot fail to sense that the American people are aware of the irony in this. However, the confusion seems to have produced frustration. Many are unhappy, and no one, including the courts, seems to know just what to do.

TO HIGHER GROUND. The courts will not supply answers to these issues. They stand, as they have stood, on the premise that public education is or can be isolated from religious education. Justice Jackson stated in a dissent (*Everson* vs. *Board of Education,* 1947):

> It (our public school) is organized on the premise that secular education can be isolated from all religious teaching so that the school can inculcate all needed temporal knowledge and also maintain a strict neutrality as to religion. The assumption is that after the individual has been instructed in

worldly wisdom he will be better fitted to choose his religion. Whether such a disjunction is possible, and whether it is wise, are questions I need not try to answer.

Justice Jackson may have been well within his prerogative in declaring that he need not answer. However, as time wears on, it becomes increasingly clear that he placed his finger precisely on the question which someone must answer if the problem is to move to higher ground.

In the opinion of this writer such a "disjunction" *is not possible.* Since it is not possible, the question of the wisdom of a religious neutrality cannot arise. There are those who argue with competence and force that a religious neutrality is possible and is wise. It is interesting that assertions to this effect made to this author in response to an earlier work[2] come from those firmly entrenched in the educational and religious establishments, and those who are most willing to concede that religious neutrality in any comprehensive program of education is impossible are, more often than not, associated with humanistic pantheism or atheism. One is left with the uncomfortable feeling that certain humanistic pantheists and atheists are fully aware of the religious intolerance propounded in recent court decisions, and are content to allow matters to rest as they presently stand.

American colleges and universities are well on their way to the severing or secularizing of their connections to religious establishments. In some cases this separation is due to changes in the style of the institution and would, therefore, have occurred without outside developments. But most colleges, sensing that government is now a new and big source of continuing support, find establishmentarian connections dangerous. Our laws have been written and interpreted in such a way that the government must collect taxes from churchgoing people, but must cleanse the money of its churchness before returning it to the people for the education of young Americans. Again, the fact that all education has religious subject matter has not been recognized. So even at the college level the theistic alternatives are being pushed into the background. Their presence is embarrassing to development officers.

Where is the higher ground upon which better practices can be founded? A fuller public understanding of the issues in the definitions

---

[2] *Religious Values in Education,* The Interstate Printers & Publishers, Inc., Danville, Ill., 1967.

the courts have rendered of the words "religion" and "establishment" would be part of the way up. More complete understanding of the various God-ideas in which people believe would certainly elevate matters further. A clarification of the anatomy of values which demonstrate the role of religious belief in the structure of a value and its expression as an attitude would also lift the issue. The higher ground will be reached when the public is prepared to answer for itself the question which Justice Jackson said he "need not try to answer." If, in the fullness of time, the public comes to an acceptance of the view that the "neutrality" and the "disjunction" to which Jackson referred *are not possible,* then the legal and administrative reforms which morality demands can be created.

Why would morality demand reform? Freedom is an indispensable condition to choice. Consequence is embedded in choice. Consequences do not inhibit a person's making a choice; he has only to be willing to accept them. Therefore, consequences do not limit freedom. On the other hand, freedom of choice is withheld when the chooser is ignorant of or not fully informed of all of his alternatives. If the alternatives implicit in the God-ideas of the American religious establishment are denied a meaningful presence or have an inferior presence in the principal learning environment of the children, youth, and young adults, then a stricture on freedom exists. It can be asserted, therefore, that the fundamental conditions necessary for free choice are not present. This can be ruled immoral on the grounds of the *categorical imperative.*[3]

One may ask how establishmentarian God-ideas could be brought into the school environment to compete with the secular God-ideas which are now there. Answers to this question, though tempting, do not fall within the plan of this essay. It is obvious that legal and administrative reforms are needed. These are easily accomplished, once the desire for them is established. Americans in the short space of time which history has thus far given them have proved to be a resourceful, energetic, and creative people. This has been said everywhere; no one has denied it. We feel safe in thinking, therefore, that once an understanding grows as to what needs doing, America will discover the means and the manner to get it done. The present difficulty is not that of *how* the thing will be done but *whether* it will be done.

As to this question, we must recognize that those who are in

---

[3] Children are regarded as means and belong not to the kingdom of ends.

kindergartens today will live a major portion of their lives in the twenty-first century. We don't know what life in this century will be like. The prophecies are so fantastic that we can only guess at its shape and substance. Issues such as genetic control of human creation, interplanetary travel, indefinite life, whether death is wanted or needed are a few of the matters which will stand to be resolved. It is not that the wisdom of the past or the strength of the past has any greatness or relevance regarding these mighty metaphysical questions. But is it moral for modern civilization, in formulating its bright new alternatives to God, to withhold those which have sustained men in former times? We cannot escape in ambiguity. The answer must be: no, it is not moral. Our children require all the light we can bring to bear on their problems. This includes the light of the past as well as the present.

ON BECOMING HUMAN

It is wise that educators occasionally contemplate infants. Rarely is the problem of education so clearly shown. The aurora of new life radiates in splendor, but the full miracle of creation is incomplete. The Creator with inscrutable wisdom leaves the completion to man. Considering his feeble powers, his interval of opportunity is brief.

For in the two short semesters of childhood and adolescence the infant must become man, not just the "hewer of wood and drawer of water" but human in the ultimate sense. Man is given the raw material out of which to make mankind. If a bad job comes of it, the mischief is his alone.

The Reverend William E. Channing, the great Unitarian, may have been contemplating an infant when he said:

> He is to be educated, not because
>   he is to make shoes, pins, and nails,
> but because he is a man.

Implicit in this observation is the suggestion that man himself is of greater importance than what he makes. Among men, who would dispute this suggestion? Indeed, many call it maxim. They rally to it; assign it the status of principle and compose epigrams in praise. Of the many contradictions in modern education the most striking by far exists in the fact that the fruits of our teaching are more often measured by the things our students can do rather than by what they are, or are becoming, as humans.

It is not by callous choice that we ignore what must certainly be the central aspect of education. I think human development is neglected because we do not understand clearly the form of knowledge with which it is concerned. What knowledge makes men better humans? We have suggested that it is not utilitarian knowledge, or at least not that alone.

Then what is it? Where is it found? What is its form? How shall it be taught? One feels within him the ancient question of Job who called out in his misery:

Man puts his hand to the flinty rock
  and overturns mountains by the roots.
He cuts out channels in the rocks,
  and his eye sees every precious thing.
He binds up the streams so that they
  do not trickle,
and the thing that is hid he brings forth
  to light.
BUT WHERE SHALL WISDOM BE FOUND?
AND WHERE IS THE PLACE OF UNDERSTANDING?
                                        Job 28:9-12

What is before us is a knowledge problem, and modern students
of education seldom study knowledge problems. But if we are to
have progress in this particular matter we must take it for what it is—a
knowledge problem. It is customary for us to speak of the foundations
of education, and we think we know a good deal about these foundations. But this occasion takes us below the foundations and here we
are amazed to find in place of bedrock certainty, the loose soil of
doubt and the shifting sand of tentative assumption.

Protagoras, the brave sophist who doubted the ancestral gods of
the Athenians, is quoted by Plato as saying, "Man is the measure of
all things." Heraclitus, the Ionian, taught that all things change.
However, Pythagoras, the Italian, found permanence in ideas. Socrates,
the relentless inquisitor, searched, as he thought, in the souls of
men for absolute meanings for abstract nouns. He stands as the
symbol of man's determination to think persistently about that which
seems apparent. Plato wrote a dialogue which has Socrates, his teacher,
in conversation with Protagoras. In this exchange the two men
discover that knowledge, whatever it is, is good. Later, in another
dialogue called the *Theatetus*, Plato established that knowledge is a
metaphysical category, a question that can never be closed.

But men have tried to close it. Some of the efforts have been
heroic. Aristotle sought to close it by defining the immanent principles
of the world as they appear in the senses of men, but these senses
have proved unreliable. He found logic is a property of reason, but
others found it not a property of nature. Augustine was contented
to begin with faith in revelation, but revelation has been found to
contradict itself. Descartes began with doubt but needed to reason
a perfect being in order to assure himself that reason itself cannot
delude him. Spinoza linked thought and substance but left no clear
indication that knowledge is of one, of the other, or, of both. Locke

was very certain that objects have qualities and these qualities can be known, but he asks that we believe that the mind which knows them is passive. Kant wrote that the objective world is represented in consciousness and we may know these representations only as they present themselves in individual experience. Pragmatists are teaching that there are processes by which nature succeeds and by which men achieve satisfaction. They insist we can know processes. Modern realists call for men to speak in logical mathematical language, believing that in this way language and reason can be the same. But of what shall we speak or reason? Existentialists declare we know only feelings so they take in sensation and idea, then turn themselves on.

Now it is conceivable that teachers and schoolmen may feel embarrassed by recognizing the knowledge problem has never been universally resolved. Knowledge is, after all, a school's stock in trade. It passes children who acquire it and fails children who do not. How can the school presume such resounding judgments when the thing they are judging is itself unknown?

The answer is that knowledge which the school claims to have is synthetic. That is to say, all cognate knowledge systems are built upon and with a *priori* synthetic assumptions. If by the test of reason, experience, evidence, coherence, or correspondence, a synthetic assumption, proposition, or postulation proves reliable or prophetic, we call it knowledge. Returning to the *Theatetus*, we might better call this "true opinion" rather than "knowledge." For what we have is a statement which is true by one of the several standards for truth which has been refined out of one of the many systems produced by western philosophers.

Now it becomes possible to say that a man does or does not have this kind of knowledge. A great deal of it exists and as time goes on the amount increases. Indeed, the increase in recent times has been so phenomenal in itself that any one man in the time of his life will acquire only a very small part of what exists. Educators have expressed concern that a man can acquire such a very small portion of the whole, and they have raised such questions as: *What knowledge is of most worth?* The question is a good one. It suggests that the great curriculum problem which stands before schoolmen is the problem of selection.

Obviously, there can be wide agreement on such things as skills of communication and other base abilities upon which social and vocational competencies are founded. Surely these can be identi-

fied and taught. So wide is the present agreement and so well
established are contemporary methods that expectations are good that
most of these skills and abilities will be taught by electromechanical
devices ere the present century runs its course. Reading specialists can
still be brought to a state of high broil over whether a phonics
program should be full, partial, or non-existent. But there are various
ways children can be taught to "read." Even now the teacher can
choose from among a set of improving alternatives. Although these
quarrels continue to be of professional interest, the bearing of such
issues on the quality of education has been exaggerated. These abilities
must be taught and taught well, and we can leave it to teachers to
choose whatever methods are best in their own hands.

Other matters of selection are not so easily resolved. We can
chorus our hope that education will somehow make a man human,
but the chorus becomes confusion and discord when we ask: What
is it to be human? What form of knowledge contributes to a humane
state of being? We have no reason to think that the acquisition of
large doses of cognate knowledge contributes to this state of being.
To be profound is not necessarily to be wise. The substance of wisdom is not in *the known* but in *the good*.

What is the source of the knowledge men need to give meaning
and purpose to existence? Various ethical systems have been developed
from realism and pragmatism; however, even on their own test of
validity they fail of usefulness, for none of these are functionally
adequate for interpreting human life or human experience in terms
which satisfy man's want for the everlasting. If human thirst can prove
the existence of water, if human hunger can prove the existence of
food, then I submit that the unquenchable human desire for insight
into the transcendent issues of life proves that such knowledge exists
somewhere—but where is it? Once again, the lament of Job:

> But where shall wisdom be found?
>   And where is the place of understanding?
> Man does not know the way to it.
>   And it is not found in the land of living.
> The deep says it is not in me,
>   and the sea says it is not with me.
> It can not be gotten for gold,
>   and silver can not be weighed as its price. . . .
> WHENCE THEN, COMES WISDOM?
> AND WHERE IS THE PLACE OF UNDERSTANDING?
>   Job 28:20

To what source will man turn for knowledge on the central issue of his life? Will he know justice by examining the law of nature? Or will he consult other sources for his ideas of justice? Will he know life as an interval in which he accepts as truth any expediency which gives pleasure and avoids pain? Or will he consult other sources for his ideas on life, the meaning of pleasure and the meaning of suffering?

Across the ages great educators have used various means to answer the questions of Job. The *humanities* are commonly conceived as a broad category of the curriculum which contains the courses usually intended to furnish men with the element of wisdom. Often, too, the *liberal arts* are said to provide these desired measures of insight. But can we assume that the content of courses commonly assigned to these fields is in and of itself humane or liberating? Obviously we cannot say this without making an assumption about what is, after all, humane, and what is liberalizing. Can a course in thermodynamics be humane? Can a course in Chaucer be technical? The answer to both of these questions can be yes, depending upon what the words mean and how the courses are taught.

Let us say that an educational experience is humane if it leads one to have a sense of the direction of the good in any of the great issues in life. Having acquired this sense, one develops an internal commitment which is religious (in the philosophical sense of the term) and, therefore, it is meaningful. Sensing the good in this way enables a man to apply any other knowledge he acquires to the conduct of his life affairs in a wise manner. Is this not wisdom? Let us say that an educational experience which brings a man to consult things other than his prejudice, greed, or ambition is liberalizing. An experience is liberalizing if it leads a man to invoke his sense of the good rather than his fear or vanity. Humane experiences develop the sense of the good; liberalizing experiences strengthen one's disposition to apply the sense of the good. Wisdom is the application of the sense of the good in the use of knowledge.

Is there content in any knowledge system which is inherently humane, liberal, and wise? Academic specialists of various types speak and behave as if there is. Teachers, they say, must have content and not method. One great college introduces its rationale on teacher education with the words, "we believe that the first essential of a good teacher is a thorough knowledge of the subject." However, we are confronted with one example after another of great teachers who know very little content. What, after all, did Socrates claim to know? What did Jesus of Nazareth claim to know? But we need not base our argument on paragons. Educational research has discovered many teachers who are rated superior by supervisors, students, and parents, who are not far advanced in any knowledge system. "My football coach," said one boy, "was my greatest teacher. He did not know much football, but he made me a man." Are we prepared now to respond that the content of football, even in small amounts, is humane, liberalizing, or wise? No, there is something in the manner, style, or attitude of the teacher. (Notice we have avoided that horrid word *method* because there is nothing to be gained by further offending the academics.)

We can lay unction upon the academics by admitting that the football coach might have been a better coach if he had known more football. We don't know, however, if he would thereby have made better men. We will freely confess that all of the superior teachers we have found who were not profound in a subject would have been even better had they known more. But would their teaching have been more humane or liberalizing? These admissions, confessions, and questions are harmless, and, indeed, they are useful if they will bring greater attention to the heart of the matter which is that the *humane or liberal influences are not products of the content but of the mode of the teaching.*

The kind of academic spigotry encouraged in modern education is not conducive to humanization. Never was there a generation so lost as our modern "test busters." Their quest for life gives increasing evidence of a resort to burlesque and trauma. They seem obsessed by shock and sensation. Youth always craves excitement, but in times when they resort increasingly to drugs, active sex, gambling, and violence, the conclusion obtrudes that their education, though content-laden, may be nonhumane and unliberal. It certainly does not reflect or produce wisdom.

What part does knowledge play in the making of a man? What is the form of knowledge that should be cast for this role? Are we to think that it is of no consequence *what* is taught and that only the manner, style, or nature of the teacher and the teaching matters? Are we to go as far as Pestalozzi in giving freedom for human interaction? We could, but we need not. Probably we should not. Our children are not destined for life in an agrarian milieu. But even so they share the same great human questions as did Leonard and Gertrude.

Certainly we can accept that all men in all times were obliged to discover what relationship they, as individuals, had with their society. We cannot doubt that they searched for *beauty* and for *truth*. All men must come to terms with *God* or with an *idea of God*. From the age of enlightenment onward, men have been obsessed with freedom and its implications. Now that men can, and do, move mountains and dry rivers, they must all try to understand what are the moral uses of nature and of the *natural world*. These issues have been called universal because they are questions which are part of every man.

Is there a form of knowledge which answers such questions? Not really. Much of that which we call knowledge has come in response to these questions; but even as this knowledge has grown, the questions remain, and each man who stands before the prospect of becoming human must answer them in his own way and for himself. Thus a *humane* educational experience deals with the *question* and helps a man in his own personal, continuous confrontation with the question. So we have, therefore, arrived at this rationale in a position which reveals that *humane* and *liberating* educational experiences are those which use content and method in dealing with the *universal questions in human life*.

So many teachers are answer-oriented rather than question-oriented. A child brings to his education these burning questions. Why not let him have the questions? Why take them away? These questions are the central thrust of his desire to know. They reflect his constant need to acquire meaning and overcome dread. The very suggestion that there is an answer which will stop his asking and satisfy his yearning is a disservice to him. We seek not to close men, but to open men. Thus education in the humanities should build upon questions, not upon answers. We should bury children in human issues rather than seek to free them from such issues.

MAN AND SOCIETY. The stage manager in the play *Our Town* steps forward to speak. Detached from the rest, he is an observer, not part of the world of players. He speaks of the people of "our town" as if they were specimens. The play itself tells of a small New England town, of a boy and a girl; they marry, have children —she dies. Interred in a cemetery with former relatives and fellow townsmen, she joins in a polylogue of the dead. She is allowed a one-day return to life. The return is painful; she complains that the living never see each other in full reality. They don't know all that is going on.

Her concerns are the timeless concerns of those in human society. Who is this person I call mother? Who is this man who calls me daughter? Who are these others? Those called negro? White? Catholic? Jew? Protestant? Who are they I call brother, friend, and neighbor? What am I to them and they to me?

Whose questions are these? Do they belong to anthropologists? Aspects of culture are relevant but the questions are not anthropological. Do they belong to sociologists? Group processes are relevant but the questions are not sociological. Are the questions psychological? Human behavior is involved but the questions are not psychological. No, these questions are not fully at home with the behavioral sciences. This is because they are the humane concerns. They are human questions. They are the kind of questions to which modern education is blind and in which modern youth is lost.

Thornton Wilder asks these questions in many ways in *Our Town*. Eugene O'Neill repeats them again and again in all of his plays. Henry Moore describes them in statuary; Picasso speaks of them with his brushes; they trouble the dreams of Lady Macbeth. Contrasting views are heard in the music of Wagner, Mendelssohn, and Gershwin. What is the form of this knowledge? Benét found the power of John Brown's body within himself. It is human knowledge, expressed in art. Where is its source? Its source is in man. Why does man have it? Because he is man.

THE NATURAL WORLD. Man is of nature; the natural world is his place of habitation. His feeble laws and governments give certain of his number the right to erect boundaries and claim personal ownership. He then sends shafts into the ground to bring forth the minerals which took millions of years to form. He sells them to other men and acquires personal wealth. He strips the forest from the slopes, rips the tops from mountains, leaving their remains strewn in the valley. The streams are swollen and yellow in the flood, and shallow and stained in the drought. The plant and fish life are gone and the surrounding soil is saturated with chemicals and waste. His smoke fills the skies, and the pollution of air, water, and land mounts.

What is man's responsibility to the natural world? Is it only to take and never replace? Only to extract and never preserve? Is this a problem of economics? Yes, there are economic questions. Does it belong to the field of chemistry, physics, engineering? Yes, all of these and others supply information which helps illuminate the problem. The question refers to all of these and none of these. Fundamentally, again it is a human question. To be asked by humans, of humans, and the answers must come from within man. Who speaks of the morality of that which I have described? Sibelius sang of it. Riley spoke of it. Sandburg wrote of it. The late Rachel Carson warned of it, and Coleridge hung about the neck of a whimsical mariner the weight of a murdered albatross. Men ravage and poets write. But man must become poetic in his deeds, else this world will one day hang killed around his neck, and the anguish of the ancient mariner will become the fate of humanity.

THE IDEA OF GOD. Another timeless question was asked by man upon the dawn of his creation. It is asked at his birth. He asks it throughout his life, he asks it at his death. Whereof am I, and wither am I going? Man wants to understand his relationship to God or, to put it in other words, his relationship to ultimate reality. Our young people are no different—they ask this same question, but answers given their forebears are not so satisfactory for them. They want to talk about God. They should talk about God. This, too, is a human question to which answers cannot be given; they must be found by the seeker.

Many suggest that the public institutions can do nothing about this and should leave it alone, ere they shall come afoul of the law, or become overmatched and bruised in an ecclesiastical contest with one or another of the religious organizations. But this is nonsense. No magistrate or churchman objects to the thing which Bach stirs within us, or complains of the transcendental musings of Emerson, or deplores the Gregorian Chant, or protests the renderings of Leonardo.

Great religious art communicates the artist's feelings about the power of God. And, if anyone does object, complain, or protest, we should stand firm on the ground that we cannot take from the field of education the only things that really matter. The questions of dogma, sacred documents, ritual, and specific beliefs are in the domain of the churches. The power, the magnitude, the completeness, and the everlasting nature of God are the domain of all humanity. It is the nature of man to ask the question, and it is the universal and, therefore, public right of man to contemplate the art which the greatest of humanity has rendered in response.

THE SEARCH FOR FREEDOM. And what does freedom mean? What are the sit-in sessions, the boycotts, and the parades all about? Do the segregationists really understand what they are withholding? Do integrationists really know what they want? Men with good sense and a common concern for humanity must ask these questions and deal with them in an atmosphere free of hostility. Our schools have become the battleground; forces on either side show little concern for the things which are taught, and act as if this issue hangs only on whether or not students of two races are together or apart. This is foolish.

Of course they belong together. But where in the history of man has anyone solved a problem by destroying a school? All human experience teaches that the problems of humanity have been caused by men of ill will and have been solved by men of good will. In the strife of the hour, there is evidence that men of good will are being forced aside and the institution which stands as the instrument of ultimate freedom, the American public school, is being damaged or destroyed in communities where it is most needed.

Any struggle for freedom is most honorable, but those who join the march might ask about the violence which brought down Caesar, raised new Caesars, and destroyed a free institution. They must learn that fighters for freedom must choose carefully the time and the place or they may destroy the very institutions in which their hope is invested. They must learn that a revolution which disposes of one tyranny must not raise another. Let them learn that the blow which leveled Becket raised the church of England, and let them ponder upon the several melancholy examples of this in the contemporary community of nations.

THE SEARCH FOR BEAUTY. What is beauty? How is it involved with the ideas of love and truth? In the *Symposium*, Plato suggests that love is of the beautiful because beauty is immortal. Aristotle finds beauty in the appearance of function. Plotinus, like Plato, sought a solution in the dynamics of emanation. For Aquinas it was an aspect of intuition, for Kant a quality of experience, and for Schopenhauer it was the objectification of will. Dewey seemed to assert it was in the public judgment. Whatever the theory, beauty stands as perhaps the sovereign humanizer of all of the forces or ideals which work upon man. One fills his life by learning to sense it, or impoverishes his life by a failure to sense it. However it comes, it is a response from within a man to something outside of him, and it is *learned*.

Men of one culture call beautiful what men of another call ugly. This teaches us that beauty is not in the nature of appearances alone but in something deeper, either in the object sensed by man or in man himself. Is this thing a universal? What is it? How can it be possessed? A man learns to perceive beauty by perceiving it, abstracting it, creating it, and questioning it. Can there be beauty in the suicide of Othello? Only if, as Aristotle suggested, we respond with our own emotions to the fullness of the tragedy, the awe, the wonder, the fear, and the irony. Thus, objectified, is not Othello himself beautiful? As one philosophizes about beauty, his sense of beauty enlarges and strengthens, and he becomes more manly than he was.

THE HUMANITIES. The humanities are not courses in the usual sense. They are excursions by discerning teachers in search of ways to bring children fully into the world of thought. They are attempts to develop in young people an awareness of higher levels of being, make them conscious of new dimensions of mind, and bring more humane substance to experience. They are endeavors consistent with liberal aspirations in education. They are efforts to bring the quality called wisdom to human experience.

They differ from courses and conventional learning units in many ways. The most important difference is that they stand apart from the utilitarian and deal with *ideas* for their own sake—not for material use, but for the purpose of developing reflectivity of mind. They bring the student into confrontation with the universal issues of human life—not for the better service of creature needs, but that the man may reach higher ground in his effort to deal with the universal questions and, thereby, make his own life a thing of greater worth.

Unlike courses, there are no fixed beginnings, no established endings, no standing exercises, no examinations and no marks or credits. All of these things diminish the humane. Indeed, an experience in the humanities wears the aspect of an open door.

There are other differences. The humanities aspire to overcome the sense of lostness which seems greatly to burden the young of our time. It proposes substance for tentative speculation and enables them to rejoice in the richness and greatness men have found in human experience. These things are done by examining the basis for human passion; by study of the quest for truth, beauty, and freedom; and by contemplation of the efficacy and omnipotence of the human mind.

The world needs greatness from America. Nothing less will suffice. We are on the road to building an Athenian culture. Schools of the future will not exist for training alone, or for the dissemination of sense knowledge alone. The schools of the future must develop greatness in our people. To do this our schools must be places where students find the greatness in humanity, where they can respond to this greatness, and feel it growing within them.

Our schools must generate a race of men such as this world has not seen before, so it will be written of the American public school that it came to fruition not as a sophistic institution responding only to the common needs and whimsies of the hour, but that it matured as man's greatest adventure in humanity. On this point rests the case for the humanities.

Job has accompanied me in this essay. Why? Because Job is every man in every age swept by doubt, rebellion, and anger against the seeming futility of human existence. At the end of this story he is contrite and humble, but he is satisfied. God commends him for his bitter questioning and assures him that his mind and intelligence can save him. God tells Job:

DECK THYSELF WITH MAJESTY AND EXCELLENCY
    AND ARRAY THYSELF WITH GLORY AND BEAUTY.
CAST ABROAD THE RAGE OF THY RATH,
    AND BEHOLD EVERYONE THAT IS PROUD, AND ABASE HIM,
THEN I WILL ALSO CONFESS UNTO THEE
    THAT THINE OWN RIGHT HAND CAN SAVE THEE.

                                                                    Job 40:10

So with the "right hand" of his own reason, his own mind, his own intellectual power, he rebuilds his faith, a faith based on internal vision and not on external sight. He no longer needs or demands a sure and certain sense knowledge on the melancholy questions of this earth. He is not a sad figure but a triumphant figure.

He stands as a symbol of man, as man alive, proud, and questioning, ultimately victorious because his mind and soul can produce vision which vanquishes doubt.

So the poet said:

> AND IN THE LAND WERE NO WOMEN FOUND
> SO FAIR AS THE DAUGHTERS OF JOB:
> AND THEIR FATHER GAVE THEM INHERITANCE
> AMONG THE BRETHREN.
> AND AFTER THIS, JOB LIVED ONE HUNDRED
> AND FORTY YEARS
> AND SAW HIS SONS AND HIS SONS' SONS,
> EVEN TO FOUR GENERATIONS.
> SO, JOB DIED, BEING OLD AND FULL OF DAYS.

Job 42:15

Part III

AUTONOMOUS IDEALS AND THE STUDY OF EDUCATION

The Asking Mind

Old woodchuck fussin' round his hole—
    He knows what he's about.
Old sage engrossed on yonder knoll—
    Perforce is filled by doubt.

The meanest critter of the wood,
    The merest meadow weed,
Are alive and alove with hardihood.
    But man must have a creed.

So only, lonely, lustful man
    (All wedges, jacks, and screws)
Must wonder at the cosmic plan
    As mortal life accrues.

He rues this age of cleverness.
    Wisdom's gone from style!
Without ideals which incandesce—
    He's blind to all worthwhile.

Will the scholar leave his knoll
    With counseling to give?
Will the woodchuck leave his hole
    And teach us how to live?

No—old woodchuck keeps aholed,
    And scholar stays aknolled.
Teachers and youth alone must find
    Values for the asking mind.

Prefatory Remarks:
The Quest for Wisdom

Centuries ago, Pythagoras, who seems to have been, among other things, a mathematician, teacher, mystic, and religious leader, took up residence in the south of Italy. He was Greek and nominally the preceptor of a society of scholars. At one time he described himself to this group as a "lover of wisdom." The Greek words he used were "philo sophia." It is easy to see how these two words became joined to form the word "philosophy" and why the classic definition of philosophy was *the love of wisdom.* Much has changed in western scholarship since philosophy became a word. Modern academicians have little to do with that which antiquity came to call wisdom. They are concerned with knowledge. There are many definitions of knowledge, and each academic discipline must work out its own.

What does any body of knowledge produced by an academic discipline contribute to the wisdom of the human race? There are various ways to answer this, but all the answers indicate that wisdom involves the applications of knowledge to the deeply based concerns of living men. In modern scholarship little is done to relate knowledge to these concerns. Each scholar remains on his own particular "knoll." The attitude of modern academic men is very like the characters in Aristophanes' burlesque of the socratics; they have their noses to the ground and their tails in the air, one end contemplating the earth and the other regarding the heavens. They do very little to help give meaning to the life which surrounds them.

Thus, the general problem of wisdom is thrown back upon those who study education. Even they are tempted to avoid it. Some education scholars would prefer to imitate other disciplines and build an exclusive "knoll" of their own. But because teachers, in the work of their lives, must face daily the new humans who are coming into being, they must also face up to man's need of wisdom. So the student of education is distinctive. He differs from the "woodchuck" who is so insensitive and underwitted that he does not know great questions exist, and he differs from the "scholar" who knows the questions exist but chooses to ignore them as he climbs upon his small domain of knowledge and shuts out the world.

No matter how far educators move in organizing a "science" of education, the metaphysics of education, like flypaper, will continue to stick to their hands. For the minds of the oncoming generation are ever asking about the values by which men are possessed. To assign meaning to life each youngster must ultimately give himself to something. Teachers must equip themselves to help the young with the search for this something. Few others, in our times, are officially concerned with this search.

SEEKERS OF WISDOM

**(On the Study of Education, Including Certain Remarks
Concerning the Joy of Academic Gaffing)**

ACADEMIC GAFFING. One good way to torment an academic man is to ask him: When you profess, what is it that you profess? Or ask him: When you study, what is it that you study? Anyone can play this game. All that is required is a mild sadism or tendency to aggression. The resulting felicity is immediately compounded by the fact that the victim himself is often pleased by the question, giving further support to the widely recognized belief that academic men are fond of being persecuted and even have a mildly suppressed death wish. Although it pains him, confuses him, and fills him with distress, an historian is always pleased to be asked: What is history? Or a mathematician is gratified to discover someone curious enough to ask: What is mathematics? Psychologists and sociologists are relatively new. Even so, such a question lays a flattering unction upon their souls. As for professors of education—they are ecstatic in their agony. Even the suggestion that education is something one might study fills them with blessed assurance.

So if you are too old for girl watching or other active sports, or if you are limited in other ways, this harmless but highly fascinating diversion is worth considering. This writer has been doing it for years. Frequently in the presence of assorted academic types at punch parties and affairs where even more profound libations are offered, I find this pursuit a welcome avolation from the hopeless small talk and shaking of hands made cold and clammy from gripping frosted drinks.

Gaffing is the name of the game. As may be obvious, the name is inspired by the malevolent hook which fishermen use to impale the unfortunate fish which have been brought boatside. Nothing could be more helpless than a fish pulled up from his aquatic sanctuary and held aloft by a diabolic curve of steel which enters him at the gills and pokes a felonious point from his gaping mouth. And there he hangs, flopping, at an unseemly angle. It is difficult to imagine a fish enjoying this sort of thing, but in the case of an academic man, this is exactly what happens. Therefore, one can go academic gaffing with a secure feeling that he is both getting and giving pleasure.

Of course, I am not alone. There are many academic gaffers. The most notorious are professors of English. Why would one wish to spend the whole of his life investigating the nuances of language if he were not planning a lifetime of forensic victories? Some years ago, while part of a delegation visiting another college, I encountered a magnificent warrior of this profession. We were attending the inevitable reception wearing our inevitable badges which proclaim both name and discipline. As he approached me I immediately sensed danger. His markings were clear. Not only did his sign say English, but his Phi Beta Kappa chain was low on his hip, as if hung down with dried scalps and shrunken heads. There was, of course, the usual perfunctory introduction and welcome. Then, said he, "I see you are in *education*. Tell me, what is it that you fellows teach after the first day?" It was magnificent; utterly magnificent. But the poor devil did not know that he had another gaffer before him. I smiled (as warmly as one can while in this kind of combat) and replied, "We teach English." All he uttered was a simple, "Oh," the like of which you might expect one female tiger to say to another female tiger upon learning she had picked up the wrong cub. Then he turned on his heel and stalked gracefully across the room. Magnificent; utterly magnificent!

Gaffing is not really quite so simple as this. It is a good thing to have on hand several "back-up" questions, preferably metaphysical so that it can be certain that a closed answer will not be given. This is especially useful in dealing with chemists, physicists, and biologists. Of course, there are outstanding exceptions but one often finds trouble with these fields because most men of science are usually quite humble. Academic gaffers always find it very difficult properly to gaff a humble man. He keeps saying there is no absolute certainty about his knowledge system and constantly suggests you ask someone who knows more about it than he does. Incredibly enough, the ones who keep saying this sort of thing are those most honored and respected in their field. Perversity of this kind makes this knowledge game the fascinating thing that it is.

The neophyte gaffer needs to be cautioned not to allow the conversation to gravitate to a discussion of credits and course titles. Nothing will more quickly convert an academic man who has been hooked by honest thoughts into a sanctimonious mountebank. Actually, what happens is that he begins substituting his metaphysics for your metaphysics. If the discussion suffers this kind of damage it is better to go back to the beginning or break it off entirely. If every history course and every literature course were suddenly to disappear, men would still have a past and still record their thoughts and feelings. It is not easy to persuade academic men to remain attentive to the field of inquiry to which they have given their lives, but the effort is worth making not only for their sake but for the sake of all of the other games we play, including the games which involve credits, courses, and graduate schools.

Probably the richest strike a bona fide gaffer can make is suddenly to be in the midst of a crowd of proposal writers. No one who is writing a proposal can afford to be humble. Not only must he tremble before his own originality and stand in awe of his own discipline, but a proposal writer must write with the conviction that his particular branch of the discipline has the power to move mountains. He must be convinced that the work he proposes to do will create serenity where there is unrest and affection where there is disaffection. Gaffing under these circumstances is the more rewarding because the victim is eager to convince the gaffer of the potence of his proposal. He is, of course, uncertain that the questioning gaffer might have knowledge of and access to a large and, to date, hidden source of funds. (Why else would he ask questions? No one does this sort of thing for his own amusement.) In addition, proposal writers are extremely sincere. Who could think a proposal writer is not?

Rich as this field is, further exploration would be a rude digression. Returning to the main line, one might ask: Was I not insincere by responding that in teaching education I also taught English? The answer is no. I do teach English. Scholars in education teach a great deal of English. They also teach philosophy, history, economics, sociology, psychology, anthropology, mathematics, and science. How can this be? As a scholar in education am I not required to respond more specifically than this? Indeed, yes. At the beginning of this discourse, I was aware that the time would come when I would have to slip the point of the hook into my own gills and move aloft on the strength of my own question. *What is the study of education?*

EDUCATION AND PHILOSOPHY. On what foundation can we place the edifice? Let us begin by rejecting a few. It would be fruitless to seek substance from etymological analysis of the verb *educare*. It does contain classical implications which are still vital. But this we call education is so pervasive, so many-fronted, that we cannot base our thoughts about the field upon what may or may not be "led out" from an omniscient soul. Similarly, we cannot build on something so ubiquitous as communications among human beings. Education certainly includes communication, but surely not all communication includes education. Learning is certainly involved in education, but this field has come to be something rather well defined in the biologic and psychologic disciplines. Teaching is often regarded as the domain of students of education. This, too, is a fallacy. Teaching, like communications, is ubiquitous. It may involve a lawyer instructing his client, a parent disciplining a child, a minister composing a sermon, a social worker visiting a family. Such possibilities are infinite in number. Perhaps then it could be confined to classroom teaching. This, too, is impossible. A student of education cannot know as much about the classroom teaching of chemistry, history, woodworking, or astronomy as those who are themselves students in these fields. Of course, a chemist can become something of a scholar of chemistry education, but he must first be a student of chemistry; and the insights he develops on the problems of chemistry education would hardly justify the presence in the academic profession of a group of scholars committed exclusively to the study of education.

What, then, do professors of education profess? I prefer to found and guide my response upon Greek philosophy, the cynosure of western scholarship. Not only does this give my discourse antiquarian respectability but any modern scholarly enterprise which aspires to more than brevet rank must demonstrate its relevance upon this shrine of western enlightenment. Pythagoras of Crotona, the *lover of wisdom*, was the man who combined the words *philo sophia* in our language into the single word *philosophy*. Pythagoras searched inside of men for wisdom. But even he was preceded in time by the Ionian scholars who sought wisdom by examining the world outside of men. Plato, the great system maker, managed to locate philosophy midway between the inward look and the outward look, between art and science. In this way philosophers could be in the tradition of either the artist who seeks within himself or the scientist who seeks outside of himself.

In this way philosophy stood ready to become the sire of any special knowledge system, and each time a dame appeared she was sired forthwith. The dames came along in the form of various scholars with special interests who discovered value in associating, specializing, standardizing, methodizing, and even at times going on to forming cants, chants, and dogmas. Ultimately the great campground which was once called the love of wisdom became divided into houses, streets, and business; we now call it the academic community. In trying to understand what it is, we seldom bother to remember what it was. This is a mistake which I wish not to make.

One house in this community, usually very disorderly, is called history. Another, usually in an uproar, is called psychology. The villa called English is by internal agreement divided up into apartments, some furnished with medieval benches, others styled with Victorian trappings, and others littered in the modern mode. These latter are often pervaded by the very distinctive odor of "pot." Some neighborhoods are more exclusive than others. A few citizen scholars are frequently out of their houses trying to make friends among the other disciplines. However, when they return to their houses it is noted that those who mingle indiscriminately are assigned to attic or basement rooms designated for metahistorians, metageologists, metamathematicians, and metaphysicians. Interdisciplinary scholars go unrewarded at home. Metaphysicians live in the attic of a neoclassical structure near the center of the community. This particular house is called philosophy and is maintained by the community in response to the same antiquarian sentiments referred to above. There is also a house called religion. Recently younger men have been going in and out of it, some of them carry signs, and frequently they visit with new-found friends in the social science neighborhood.

There is also a house called education. It seems an object of much anger. A few of the windows are broken because some members of the community cannot pass it by without throwing a stone. Nevertheless, it stands there and seems to grow bigger every year. Why is this? What manner of scholars live together in there? What do they do?

Part of the answer rests in what has occurred in philosophy and in religion. The rest of it lies in what is happening and what will soon be happening throughout the entire institutional order. Ever since the end of the Second World War, reputable philosophers have been writing about what is happening to philosophy. It would be presumptuous to attempt in so short a space to either summarize or epitomize this cascade of splendid thought. However, it seems fair to report that the most realistic, which is not to say the most appealing, portions of this discourse hold that philosophy is giving itself to the so-called practical affairs of men. This is to say that it is ministering to the language and the thought of extant knowledge systems by improving the logic of information systems and inventing quasi-mathematical languages for near absolute communications. Of course, there are those who maintain custody of the remarkable body of ontological thought which men of western scholarship accumulated across twenty-five hundred years. These are the metaphysicians who live in the attic. Occasionally there is a new study of Spinoza or Locke. Commentaries on Kant and Rousseau are still popular. But, in general, philosophers have closed this front, believing that moral substance, if it exists, is not knowable in any generally acceptable way. Definitive life judgments in these matters, therefore, are beyond the reach of rational or empirical inquiry.

This represents more than just a change in the house of philosophy. From the Greeks to the dawn of the present century, men held that practical concerns are *inferior* and that concerns which deal with the eternity of being are *superior*. Philosophy, therefore, seems to have de-emphasized the aspect of its life which by long tradition has been devoted to the *love* or *search for wisdom*. Contemporary philosophy has little to say about the purposes which give direction and meaning to human activity.

Across the centuries religion and philosophy had been close neighbors. During the Middle Ages they lived together and retained what little western man could retain of the scholarly traditions of Biblical and pagan antiquity. Now that part of religion which remains close to philosophy takes the tone of *theological apologetics*. The rest of it seems to be riding off in several directions. Many professionals in religion, that is to say *the clergy*, find the role traditionally assigned to them in the institutional order as a convenient ingress to contemporary social problems. Perhaps this is to praise them, for these problems are severe and demanding. But, on the other hand, some of these problems have spiritual origins. Where, then, does one best minister to a man's spirit? Where is it best to stop a waterfall? At the bottom? Or at the source?

No one needs to go off searching for the gap which has been left by this redeployment of philosophy and religion. It yawns before us like the open sky. If, as John Dewey suggested, "Wisdom differs from knowledge in being the application of what is known to the intelligent conduct of the affairs of human life,"[1] then who is concerned with that which we call wisdom? Men, of course, have not ceased loving wisdom. But which among the modern academic disciplines will openly confess that its primary concern is that *superior reality* which we call wisdom? Is the love of wisdom out of vogue in the academic profession? Indeed, it may be out of vogue, but it is not absent. It has been suggested that philosophy, that is to say philosophy in the traditional sense, is the general theory of education. Or, to use Dewey's metaphor, "Education is philosophy in working clothes."

PURPOSE AND PROCESS. Now this suggests a syntax for educational scholarship but does not describe the structure of the scholarly enterprise in education. Certainly many, perhaps most, students of education deal very little with academic philosophy as such. But this does not mean they do not concern themselves with what is wise. Perhaps it would be a good thing if more education scholars were trained in philosophy; but, clearly, the events of our times argue that intense study of philosophy by students of education is not a necessary thing. Students of education do not necessarily look at wisdom *per se.* Instead, they look at the institutions which men erect in order to bring wisdom to their lives. What are these institutions? They are schools, governments, families, churches, civic groups, social groups, political groups, and organizations given to medicine, charity, and law. Men can be seen everywhere, working within institutions, articulating purposes and instituting processes, and trying to understand both in the very broad context of bringing greater wisdom into the lives of those whom they reach. Here, then, are words which offer a structure to the study of education. Education is the *study of purpose and process in the institutional order.*[2]

Within the present year lawyers, nurses, dentists, clergy, social workers, health officials, conservation leaders, school board members,

---

[1] John Dewey, *Philosophy of Education* (Ames, Iowa: Littlefield Adams & Company, 1956), p. 7.

[2] *Educational research,* its methods, standards, and modes, is given only passing reference here. However, scholars of education are uncovering important information about teaching and other institutional processes by application of relatively new empirically based analytical procedures which are generically called *educational research.* This will be discussed in the subsequent essay.

school business managers, and several other professional kinds have enrolled in courses or programs in schools of education. This listing is in addition to the numerous teachers and school specialists which constitute the bulk of students enrolled in education courses and programs. One plain fact of academic life today is that the institutional order is massive, active, and growing, and no modern division of university scholarship faces up to the whole of it except education.

This fact did not result from the aggression of educational scholars. It resulted from the withdrawal of other disciplines. I wish I could recall for you the hundreds of times in the past six years that I have been approached by representatives of one or another institution which stands cogent and needed in the American civilization with a request that their group be included in the operations of the School of Education. More often than not, they began their request somewhere else, but they found they could not be helped. So they came to education; and more than occasionally they found what they had been seeking.

In part this suggests that the modern academic colossus called education came into being because other disciplines had not taken on certain jobs. To a certain extent, this is true. But it would be a mistake to think that other disciplines really had a choice. In most cases they would have had to abandon their current standards and objectives in order to minister to the educational needs of new or emerging human service professions. Law and medical schools have remained very narrow in their concerns, but we can certainly sympathize with their obsessive interest in training superior practitioners.

Education, itself, however, needs to consolidate. It would be better if education could define its structure as the *purposes and processes of institutions of learning*. This would help greatly, but before it can be done there must be an expansion of other professional schools. I can assert, on the strength of my own experience, that there is pressing need for other professional schools.

It is very interesting to consider the study of education as it is conducted in undergraduate colleges. Most education courses at this level are designed for those who expect to become classroom teachers. Classroom teaching is a special kind of vocational skill associated with the current styles of elementary and secondary education in the United States. Now that teachers colleges are, or soon will be, a thing of the past, the bulk of these teachers will come from liberal arts colleges, both public and private.

There are two standing fallacies here that should be examined. The first is that vocational study of this kind is not *humane*. No one really questions the humane insights demanded of a modern classroom teacher or suggests that these insights come from education courses alone. The principal sorrow is that so many education courses are reduced to prescriptions and so many elementary and secondary schools are run by prescriptions that undergraduate study in education is seemingly nonhumane. If an education course is patterned on the authentic life of a modern classroom, then it would be of humane value to any who take it, even if they never teach a day.

The second fallacy is that persons who have had undergraduate study in education which is designed to prepare them to become classroom teachers are, by virtue of this study, scholars in education. On the contrary, they have not even begun the systematic study of education. The objective of preparing for classroom teaching in the space of 18 undergraduate hours demands that disciplinal concerns be omitted. It would not really matter to the professional scholar in education if undergraduate courses did not carry the title "education." They deal with a very specific set of skills which might be summarized by the term classroom didactics, but they do not usually lead far in the direction of useful insights of the purposes and processes of the institutional order. However, there are some undergraduate colleges which offer good courses in the History or the Philosophy of Education. Occasionally a study called the Social Foundations of Education can rise to these heights. Men have been known to make their Psychology of Education into a lively and rigorous course. Where this happens, students from all over the college flock to it. They sense its vitality and its value in filling the great gap which was opened when philosophy and religion abandoned the grounds upon which men stood by openly proclaiming themselves to be *lovers of wisdom*.

EDUCATION AS A TRANSDISCIPLINE. Now I return again to my assertion that I teach English. The assertion was not presumptuous, at least it was not so intended. If, as I have claimed, education is the study of purpose and process in the institutional order, and if the purpose of the institutional order is to bring wisdom into the conduct of human affairs, then education students are in their proper roles as seekers of wisdom. There are many possible sources for wisdom. In the study of educational philosophy we attempt to take note of all the best that has been thought and said by western man, Language is the mode by which thought is formed and by which thought is expressed. Students of education must learn to deal with ideas. Therefore, they must learn to use the handles and harnesses by which western philosophers have managed ideas. Students of education work in various ways to help the institutional order with its constant examination of purposes. Therefore, the language by which the ends and values of western man are, and have been, expressed is an object of my professional interest. This kind of language study is a means and not an end, but this does not devalue either me or the effort I make.

Likewise, I am a student of history. Western ideas have been expressed in places and times. Therefore, they have two forms of relevance. The first is the relevance they had to their own time and the second is the relevance they have to modern and, by implication, to future times. These two forms of relevance have both independent and contingent relationship. Students of education who are at work in the institutional order must understand ideas in these historical contexts. A professional cannot serve his institution well unless he can sense its past. This means more than knowing a few dates and names. It means he must sense *how the spirit of his institution has moved through time.* Thus armed, he can help his institution to understanding its purposes and how its purposes will register upon the future.

Sometime ago I was in conversation with a retiring president of a great urban university which had served that city well. I asked him if it was possible that his successor, whoever it might be, would change the direction of the institution from its present intense commitment to the service of urban needs. He replied: "He would have to change the history of this institution; no one can do that." I thought his answer adequate. This particular president was a student of history. Again, this kind of historical study is instrumental and not for the sake of history *per se.* But this does not make his interest in history any less than that of the most dedicated historian.

Institutions have processes as well as purposes. They are not really separable, but it is possible to think of them as separate things even though one is inevitably imbedded in the other. Processes involving human beings must take into account human behaviors, characteristics, and relationships. Processes involving groups must necessarily involve tendencies, traits, and procedures. Humans in groups produce something called culture. Therefore, the student of education must study the applications of psychology, sociology, and anthropology to the extant processes of the institutional order. These behavioral science foundations are essential to educational scholarship. One who is deficient in these applications is simply not ready to work in the field.

Thus the foundation of a man's preparation to become a seeker of wisdom through professional study of the purposes and processes of institutions consists of philosophy, history, psychology, sociology, and, perhaps, anthropology as applied to the institutional order. Beyond this he needs to be trained in the special methods and standards which are recognized in the growing discipline of educational research, and he must be trained in the specific service to the institutional order which stands as his professional specialty. Those who have this kind of training are increasing in demand. They are deliberately trained as perceptive generalists who can put an institution on its feet by aligning its processes with its clearly and constantly articulated purposes. It is true that some men can do it without this kind of training. But this is also true of any other human enterprise. A gifted leader with powerful intuition and blazing insights can do the things for which most others require training and experience, and one can always point to examples of academic administrators who, without prior training, led an institution to greatness. But there are not enough men of this kind to man the many key stations in the institutional order. This is why a leading official of one of America's great philanthropies called a school of education, saying, "I have looked all around; our men need some of the things you are doing for your people. Can you help us?"

When I turn my thoughts to my own field, asking what it is that prompts such requests, I cannot attribute it to any special brilliance of education scholars. Neither can I attribute it to exotic new discoveries in educational science or technology. We are not any more efficient, devoted, or discerning, than anyone else. I am convinced it is because we are the only significant discipline in the academic profession which studies the institutional order itself and thereby gives direct support to the effort of institutions to bring wisdom into human affairs. There are many ways to say it. In modern times few people seem attracted to simple statements, but we know it wise to state things as simply as they can be stated. What is the study of education? The study of education is the search for wisdom. This is the gift an education scholar can bring to his civilization. It is a

mission worthy of his very best effort. Knowing this, he needs no
further exhortation.

ON EDUCATIONAL RESEARCH

THE SEARCH FOR KNOWLEDGE. Graduate students and faculty constantly discuss the question, "What is research?" In my own student days this query was made to me a number of times. Once it was asked by a professor whose specialty was history of education. How clearly I recall giving my answer: "a quest for knowledge." The man solemnly nodded and the discussion moved to other matters. Surely the answer was adequate. What more can be said?

I was not to know "what more" until much later in life. The time came for a thorough reading of the Platonic dialogues. In the course of this reading I discovered the *Theatetus* in which Socrates asks a young Athenian the question, "What is knowledge?" The question is never resolved and the two-hour conversation ends with the teacher frustrated and the student confused. Initially, the reader is brought to wonder why the *Theatetus* was written. Later, understanding comes. The failure of the *Theatetus* to reveal the nature of knowledge was not a philosophic debacle but a work of surpassing genius. In it Plato established knowledge as a metaphysical category. After 2400 years of western scholarship, it still is.

Thus, it turns out that my simple answer, "a quest for knowledge" was nonsense, and my first reaction was that the professor was a fool to accept it. But this professor was not a fool. Even then he knew *The Dialogues* better than I ever will. As I now reflect on his nature I realize that, indeed, he was not a fool but a very wise man who had acquired a then unappreciated tolerance of young fools.

This does not mean that a man cannot give a meaningful definition of knowledge. Men do. But every definition of knowledge departs from a metaphysical assumption which is either stated in the definition or implied by it. In making a claim of knowledge, a man either consciously or unconsciously establishes a frame of reality within which that which he asserts as knowledge can stand as knowledge. By frame of reality is meant the metaphysical assumption on which the knowledge can be based. When a man says, "I know

that I am alone," his assumption is that his perceptions reveal to
him all of the reality that is around him and that appearances do
not in any way deceive him. But he can never escape from the
ultimate question: Is any of us ever really alone?

This is the sort of thing which makes producing scholars so
impatient with metaphysicians. The latter are not content to allow
even the most self-evident knowledge claims to stand unquestioned.
The man who knows he is "alone" is asked to identify the category
of self-theory which he believes or assumes true. If he responds to
questions about this he soon finds the aloneness claim is subject to
interpretations which vary as to whether his self-theory is materialist,
dual-idealist, interactionist, epiphenomenalist, occasionalist, or something else. Is he a manifestation of God's perception? Does his being
have only a single aspect? What is meant by consciousness? Are
all men part of a single intelligence?

Again, the lesson of the *Theatetus* is that no single theory
can "bring the many sorts of knowledge under one definition." The
metaphysician wants his colleagues to understand that his contribution can throw light upon the many sorts of knowledge possible and
thereby induce understanding and tolerance of all. But, alas, instead
of tolerance for all there is only a condescending tolerance of
metaphysics, and at times not even that.

In my recent work I have not found an article of knowledge
without its metaphysical assumption. Even Descartes' *cogito ergo
sum* implies that "thought," which gives each man an individual
existence, could be somehow connected to a single race mind as some
modern pragmatists have suggested, a microcosmic aspect of an
absolute mind as Hegel seemed to assert, the perception of God as
Berkeley apparently believed, or simply that there is something that
thinks. There appears to be no escape from the conclusion that all
knowledge is contingent. Knowledge must be based on an assumption
about reality. Each article of knowledge is as secure as the assumption
on which it is based is defensible.

THE METAPHYSICAL ASSUMPTION. Now as I observe the issues
among scholars within and between disciplines the conviction grows
that the differences more frequently arise from differing metaphysical
assumptions than from disagreements about research methods. There
are, of course, differences about the latter, but these are far more
easily resolved than differences stemming from dissimilar assump-

tions. In fact, the walls that have grown between the disciplines have been erected in order that scholars can stand peacefully on the chosen foundations of their knowledge-making systems. The clearness of this will readily be seen by anyone who attempts to understand an interdisciplinary operation.

There is never peace within a discipline. Consider history. Here is encountered a bewildering host of labels which identify categories of historians. There are relativists, positivists, descriptivists, empiricists, revisionists, and objectivists. Some, like Hegel, seek to discover spirit in time against a general theory of expressed will and emerging freedom. Others, like Gibbon and Toynbee, undertake examinations of empirical evidence which in turn seems to obtrude general historical laws upon the reluctant but objective mind. Some, like Neibuhr, describe the events of their civilization from the relevance of institutions such as the Christian Church. (This kind of history is very like that done by educational historians.) Still others posit a general theory of society such as economic determinism and interpret human events in the light of that theory. One is forced, therefore, to conclude that any history department which contains more than one producing or teaching historian is apt to be, in itself, a kind of interdisciplinary center. These differences include, of course, differences in method. However, these are not the important differences. When one historian goes about saying that another historian's work is not really history, he is not just despairing the other man's methods; he also disputes his assumptions.

Some historians are in the humane tradition while others range over to the social science. Here we find another assortment of fellows and factions. It is difficult to gain a tenable understanding of what is going on in social science. In recent years the term behavioral science and its cognates have acquired a fashionability. The term *behavior* offers some help because it obviates the necessity of establishing an assumption about the reality of society. It suggests the scholar will look at what people do and record it. However, no record of human behavior can be developed outside of a theoretical framework which gives it syntax. Without the framework there can be only random notations which wear the aspect of chaos.

The social scientist looking at human behavior comes loaded with his premise about the nature of man. Some consider him a social vocal phenomenon, others see him as a configuration of primordial appetites or drives with a capacity for rationality; to others he is an expression of an ideal. Most of them want to say that he has problems or needs, and they use these as a starting point of producing "knowledge." Now all of these things presuppose a belief about what a man is, and, like the man who says he is alone, his knowledge claim is incomplete without its metaphysical base.

Description is the oldest tradition in materialistic science. It is said that Aristotle, while on one of his honeymoons (he is supposed to have married twice) made a collection of sea shells, carefully classifying his specimens and describing each category. His passion for order evidently exceeded his passion for other things. The disciplines of descriptive science made possible the earth and life sciences that contribute so much to our present era. There appear to be no clear patterns in the growth of method within disciplines. Most begin in description; at some point experimentation, mathematical analysis, and predictive generalities appear; but all rests upon good description. Where description is poor, the science founders. Astrology and phrenology were descriptive disciplines founded on metaphysical assumptions which have been rejected by the academic profession. Yet the description that was done in these fields was similar to that of other disciplines. What was it that finally revealed these to be pseudo-sciences? Evidently their descriptive knowledge had not *the potential for predictive generalities.*

Further speculation on the role of metaphysics in knowledge theory is tempting but not within the plan of this essay. The specific purpose here is to illuminate certain issues in educational research. A school of education is a transdisciplinary center, made so by virtue of the variety of metaphysical assumptions on which students of education base their work. And, as expected, the various scholars offer up their own definitions of knowledge and consequent views on the research which produces it.

OPERATIONISM. This returns us to a more detailed consideration of the behavioral sciences. It is in this area that logical positivists have attempted to discover a theory for a science of education. The history of this effort dates from the dawn of the century. Many notable efforts have been made, and although progress has not been so swift and certain as we may wish, there has been progress. In 1927 Bridgman offered a pragmatic method of inquiry into the meaning of concepts in physics. Subsequently, his method was called operationism and became the object of many commentaries, favorable and otherwise. However, in its elementary form its potential as a foundation for research in education could not be exploited.

Tate,[1] in an effort to remedy this defect, offered a tightly reasoned statement of the operational principle with particular reference to a science of education. He proposed the following four corollaries of this principle as a basis for improving research in education:

First Corollary. Problems or questions which are reduced to performable or conceivably performable operations have unambiguous meanings.

Second Corollary. Problems or questions which are reduced to performable operations can be dealt with in science.

Third Corollary. Whatever is reliably observed is known, in terms of the operations and conditions of its observation.

Fourth Corollary. Whatever is known is non-trivial to the extent that it explains or predicts events of public concern.

There has been and is pronounced disagreement as to whether or not the operational principle is in itself a metaphysical assumption. Likewise there would be disagreement as to whether the aforementioned derivatives of this principle contain subject matter which is metaphysical. I am disposed to believe they do. However, I am inclined to agree with what seems to be Professor Tate's assertion that it does not matter. Operationism presents educational science with defensible standards of rigor (which is to say, clarity). and high standards of rigor are conducive to the improved development of any knowledge system.

What can it teach us to do? First, to observe and record our problems with greater precision; second, to define the meaning of problems or questions in terms of human experiences or operations; third, to recognize that a concept is synonymous with a corresponding set of operations; fourth, to recognize that solutions are verified in terms of what they accomplish (that is to say, one aims where he hits); and finally, to understand that the test for triviality is the public concern.

The frame of reality is pragmatic. As such it turns aside from the a priori; it avoids the endless ambiguities of goal making, and it forces the scholar to remain in the domain of experienceable processes

---

[1] Tate, Merle, Operationism, Research, and Education, Harvard Educational Review, 1950, Vol. XX, No. 1, pp. 11-26.

wherein and whereby his performances can be judged and the stand-ards of his work more uniformly recognized.

The operational researcher does not exhaust himself by the quest for universals, nor does he wish to devote time to arguments as to their existence or non-existence. He deals with a set of opera-tions. In the case of a pig, the operationist is not concerned as would be the Platonist with the idea of *pighood*. Likewise he would not take interest in the essence of *pigness* which interested Aristotle and later the scholastics. The operationist is concerned with *piggism* which we might call the set of operations an object goes through when being a pig. (He grunts, rolls in the mud, digs with his nose, and eats all you give him.) The operationist concedes that the ideas or essences (pighood, pigness) may have reality, but he can *see* the operations of that we call a pig (and in this example he can also smell them). As to whether or not piggism is or is not a universal, I am inclined to think that a reasonably good metaphysician could demonstrate that it is a species of universal.

The word "pig" is not a good nor a fair example. However, it has the virtue of being vivid. More to the point is "intelligence." Here the operationist does not seek the conventional universal. His stand is that intelligence is the set of operations which are per-formed in determining intelligence. It is nothing more. It is an oversimplification to say that intelligence tests test whatever they test. They do, of course, but there are also the elements of reliability and of prophecy which are expectations inherent in the operations. The investigator is free to work with intelligence tests without first devoting his life to a study of a universal meaning for intelligence. He can simply ask: "What does measured intelligence predict about other operations such as school achievement?"

Tate and others seem to have made the point that working within this tight frame of reality (or set of assumptions) we have the possibility for a science of education. Those who choose to work in the domain of educational purpose will be greatly strengthened by having available the reliable knowledge with prophetic value which can only be produced by those working in the frame of reality which operationism delineates. It is to be hoped, of course, that operationism can expand its frame. Some students of education are now demanding that educational goals be stated in "behavioral" terms. Otherwise, they say, no one can ever know what they mean, and science cannot approach them.

CONCERNS WITH OPERATIONISM. Before moving to a broader view of educational research, it is appropriate to record two concerns about operationism worth noting. The first is that it is nonteleological, and, therefore, the problems and concerns upon which it thrives must be fed in from sources external to the frame of reality in which it exists. It has the capacity to demonstrate, clarify, and predict. However, in the vogue it currently enjoys, implications are often voiced that out of this educational science will come the information which tells schools what they *ought* to be doing. And yet, oughts have been ruled out of operationism by those who defined it. *This should be made clearer than it has been.* The second concern relates to the rhetoric of the scientist. By definition, operational language is free of universals (or contains universals of a kind which is different[2] from those used in conventional discourse). But everywhere in educational conversation today we find bright, alert young men using operational language as if it contained universals of a conventional sort. The result to the listener is double-talk in the most classic sense of the term, and the effect on his reason is nonsense.

In the latter connection I recently encountered a researcher who wanted to discuss a set of operations we have all understood to be achievement standards. However, he wanted to avoid the conventional universal of the word "standard" because of a sensitivity his audience had to that word. (He was right about the sensitivity.) So he described his work as establishing "base lines." When, in the questioning period, this was shown to be unsatisfactory, he offered "bench marks." When plied with more questions he was brought to admit that the operations he described were in other times and places called achievement standards. Now how can this happen? If the nominal aspects of a language do not contain or refer to universals (or do not contain or refer to universals of a conventional sort), then the user may take license to invent or adapt any descriptive word to designate a set of operations which exists nowhere except in his dreams.

Instead of rigor this often comes out to be a burlesque of rigor. Instead of communication we have pseudocommunication. Men who have observed little or nothing of which they speak stand liberated from the substance out of which mortals develop conversation. With

---

[2] It seems an operational concept must forever be generic. If a concept is defined by a set of operations, an operation removed from or added to the set must, therefore, change the concept.

this rarefied rhetoric they score a forensic triumph and call it research. As this tendency commingles with competition for funds and public acclaim, we are often served a verbal mixture that sends us in search of the nearest sewer.

If rules are enforced to control distortion and inflation in language, the operational principle, augmented by the Tate corollaries, offers students of education an excellent prospect for rigor in educational scholarship. Is it the only form for acceptable research in education? No, but we must, in all honesty, concede that it is more advanced in this regard than are the others which are presently in use. Whatever human value rigorous thinking offers to our students, this value comes to them when their research is consummated under these standards.

We are accustomed to classifying research in various ways—historical, philosophical, descriptive, etc. I have noted that education professors are prone to become animated in the defense of one or another of these classifications. Occasionally, we hear one of the specialists in the empirical-behavioral-operational mode say *these others are not research*. This strikes me as extremely surprising because, having renounced conventional universals in favor of a set of operations, the operationist is bound to accept as his concept of research *the set of operations one performs in doing research*. The only thing that saves him from the high school principal who wants to count the number of blue-eyed blondes in the tenth grade is Professor Tate's fourth corollary on triviality. Even this does not demote it from being research. It simply establishes that it is trivial research. Moreover, authoritarian pronouncements of this kind are also surprising in that operationism purports to renounce *a priori* or *authoritarian* positions. How, then, is an authoritarian statement about what other modes of inquiry are or are not, supportable?

WHEN IS RESEARCH RESEARCH? It isn't. But aside from the needless friction, heat, and confusion such assertions create within a school of education, they are of little importance. The important matter, and the central point of this essay, is the matter of rigor. One must build his scholarship on a tenable metaphysical assumption, and he must use defensible methods; but the key to whether or not it is acceptable as doctoral research is not assumption, not method, but rigor.

In an examination of a proposal for doctoral research it is the responsibility of the student to offer to the committee which examines the proposal his views on the levels of rigor which are implicit in his method and to demonstrate that the work he proposes to do is at a level of rigor appropriate to the doctor's degree. By this is meant the metaphysical assumptions must be clear, the logic of justification coherent, and every apparent source of error recognized and controlled by the best methods available. There are, of course, other issues such as its relevance to education and its triviality or importance, but if a design fails of rigor the design should fail of our acceptance regardless of how relevant or important it may seem.

We may need help from professional philosophers on language, value, and descriptive studies and help from professional historians on historical studies because we don't know as much about rigor in these fields as we do in the empirical-behavioral-operational modes. However, this does not alter in any way the responsibility of educational scholarship to proceed on these less familiar grounds. If studies in philosophy, history, or sociology add to what can be known about the *purposes* or *processes of educational institutions,* these scholars in education are obliged to undertake them and, so doing, meet the standards of scholarship put forward by those disciplines.

Finally, the word "research" will continue giving us trouble unless we learn to use it in the analogical sense. By this I mean the doctrine of "analogical predication" which occurred to Aquinas and was amplified by Cajetan. It is a complex issue, but the basic idea is simple. The word research to its various practitioners is not used *univocally* (i.e., with exactly the same meaning). Nor, on the other hand, is it used *equivocally* (i.e., with wholly different and unrelated meanings), as for example, "ball" refers to a gay social occasion and also to the instrument used in a game. (Try the various equivocal manifestations of the word "bat.") There is a definite connection, therefore, between the principal who is counting blue-eyed blondes and a doctoral candidate who is dealing with a thesis through a tight experimental design.

The term research is used neither univocally nor equivocally but analogically. As such, it is representative of a hierarchy of rigor and relevance in educational scholarship. In the case of my oft abused researching principal, the term research is analogically downward on the standards of rigor and relevance. In the case of the doctoral student it is analogically upward. In the vernacular of our era there are "drinks" and there are *drinks.* No one owns either the word drink or the word research. A faculty member who reads widely may be researching at one station on the hierarchy while another who is formulating improved or stronger elements in the knowledge system we call his "discipline" is at a higher station. The former may speak of his research to the Rotary Club; the latter will record his in select journals. The hierarchy is there and we all know it.

So our question is not "What is research?" but "What is rigor?" In the case of doctoral proposals the responsibility falls upon the student and his advisor to establish that enough rigor is there for the thesis to stand. My basic position is that all doctoral studies in education will contain some metaphysical subject matter. However, to me, this has not been and will not be an issue. I have been and am concerned with rigor and not with the method or modality of the research. Education in its broadest sense is a mission to bring wisdom into human affairs through the workings of institutions. Educational scholarship is, therefore, the study of institutions engaged in this effort. It is not, however, an analysis of institutional processes alone. To have any meaning, scholarship must look beyond the institutions to the wisdom the institutions seek to incarnate. Operationism, therefore, cannot be the single source of standards for educational scholarship. Studies in education must continue to deal with the values and ends of western civilization. Not everyone needs to do this sort of thing, but very little is happening outside of education, and the tragedy would be compounded if educational scholarship in its quest for an educational science ceased to concern itself with the purpose for civilization.

Part IV

THE ALIENATION OF INSTITUTION AND IDEA

The Welter of the World

Have you ever seen:
    A tiger in a cage,
    A dog confined by leash,
    A man behind the bars,
    A child repressed in school?

Have you ever heard:
    The cadence of a drill,
    The whistle of a guard,
    The summons of a bell,
    The rattle of a chain?

Can you understand:
    A cage belies a bird,
    A leash denies a dog,
    A chain distorts a man,
    And drill unmans a child?

They say that change must ever come
    And so it ever shall.
    For institutions made by men
    Offend the heaven of ideas
    Which came before us all.

So thus the ceaseless change flows on.
    For manhood men will strive.
    For childhood children aim.
    All things work to be themselves
    And clash with what restrains.

Prefatory Remarks:
The Struggle Toward First Principles

Some who have noted this writer's tendency to assert first or *a priori* principles have complained of this as a seeming contradiction with his oft stated support of the existentialist view that man arrives in the world with his essence undetermined. This is not a contradiction. It is simply acceptance of a belief that man is free and is a chooser, and *this is the first principle of man*. As part of this I also agree that his existence includes pathos and dread. However, these do not eliminate his choosing; on the contrary, they make the necessity of his choosing the compelling thing that it is.

Now a man who lives with others, even in a society of autonomous individuals, must have institutions. Institutions protect, feed, and clothe him. They educate him, govern him, perpetuate him, and assist him in his search for a personal truth. In order to do this institutions must, to some extent, oppress him. The degree to which he can forbear this oppression is related to how closely these institutions are aligned to the purposes for which he understands they exist.

For example, when Thoreau states he wants a government that governs not at all, one might accuse him of stating nonsense. However, on further reflection we can understand that Thoreau means that the first principle of man is to *be free* and the first principle of government is to function so as to *keep him* free. This is the ideal of government. Likewise, man as a chooser is forced to seek truth. If a university is to serve him in this regard, then the first principle of the university is the *search for truth*. This is the ideal of a university. In similar fashion all of man's other institutions grow out of his aspiration to actualize his freedom to choose the ideals which will then possess him and give meaning to his life.

But, alas, because institutions are man-defined, man-formed, and man-operated, interpretation and error are ever present. So the work of redefinition, reform, and revision goes ever on. This we see as change, inevitable and ubiquitous change. Occasionally an institution such as a government, a university, an economic system, or a social system gets so far out of line as to be perverse. It expressly denies the freedom it was made to foster.

127

In such cases man rebels, and when men rebel together there is revolution. Recently there has been a good deal of this in western civilization. Rousseau put the general complaint succinctly in a memorable sentence: "Man is born free but is everywhere in chains."

Those who teach should meditate about teaching. One who does the work of his life as a teacher should understand that the *purposes* (ideals) of the institution which employs him and the *purposes* (ideals) of the parents, the children, and, indeed, of man himself set the moral foundations for the teacher's work, determine the spirit of his operations, and shape his own rights and responsibilities. One who has not reflected at length on these purposes will probably not understand any of these matters. I have seen the consequences of this all too often. The work such a teacher does fails to provide him with the satisfaction that work should give a man, and the institution is taken that much further off its course by having as part of it one so erratic as not to know what he is doing.

THE UNIVERSITY AS WILL
AND IDEA

THE PROMETHEAN SPIRIT. Often as I cross the grounds and walk the halls of a great university, I am filled by the long breath of wonder. What is the source of this awe? Why am I stirred by this place? The architecture is no more than commonplace in a civilization which raises towers of business to the base of clouds and swings bridges like hammocks across great waters. No, it is not the surroundings alone which bring this suspiration within me. Could it then be the massive role that this and its kindred institutions have in shaping the contemporary affairs of men? Again, no; there are great chambers of law and charity, medicine and industry, commerce and government, wherein this feeling never swells. It is not the habitation or name, nor is it the exertions of its residents in behalf of modern society. There are many places made by human hands which answer even more strongly to the daily needs and wants of men. There is something more, something unseen, unheard. Perhaps we can call it spirit.

How does it grow? Where does it dwell? Constantly in American universities it is tissued over by the uncomely growths of bureaucracy, hippodrome, and extravaganza. But it is constantly there, generating a special sense of restlessness to those in its presence, and when these tissues of artifice become plates of oppression it explodes. Like a manacled giant, it heaves, bursts its chains, strains, and rises. Then, as if nauseated by a weight which lies dead in its stomach, it strains, convulses, and sickens. A university in these straits is not pleasant to see. But ere long the disgorgement ceases, and this living thing settles back asserted and cleansed, unseen, and once again unheard; but everywhere men are astounded at the force and violence of the eruption. This eruptive spirit which dwells constantly within a university is not subject to profanation. It will not forbear corruptions. It suffers them only briefly; then it throws them off. It will endure the vanities of mankind only so long. Men of great wealth have founded universities; but when the university spirit comes to dwell within new walls, the founders are soon chagrined to find the spirit loves them less and other things more. Wealth, it seems, can implant a great university, but wealth can never buy a great university. Men cannot possess a university.

How can we express the inexpressible? How can we compare the incomparable? How can we conceive this marvelous thing? It is not a property of one man. It is more than the bylaws of corporate existence. No rule can be written to express it. It stands sovereign to law. It is an autonomous ideal, an ideal reflected on the "wall of the cave" as a community of scholars—seeking, searching, asking, and disputing. We recognize it where we see it. But its essence is more than what is seen and heard. When was the university born? Perhaps it was that colossal moment in man's distant, dim, and unremembered past when the first creature of the homo sapiens formed upon his lips the question: "Why?" Perhaps the era of its infancy was that long and violent epoch when groups of men looked to the elements, the animals, and the oceans to discover their own cosmic name, address, and destiny. It began and continued as an indomitable drive to know more and to know better. It became the quest for Truth for its own sake with no other end or motive. Must there be a Truth in order that men can seek it? Perhaps there is a Truth, perhaps not. However, the *quest is real,* and the commitment is real, and men *feel* as if there is a Truth. There are various ways of describing man's origin, but no better moment can be found than that divine instant when the flame of Truth first kindled and flickered. It was the birth of Mind, and the university was there.

If one stands upon the Acropolis, that once great citadel which still rises majestically above the modern city of Athens, his guide can point out landmarks of the civilization which first brought western man to levels of philosophy. Far beyond the Dipylon Gate, beyond ruined walls, can still be seen the grove of the Academy. Here, tradition holds, Plato taught geometry and philosophy. There, by a shrine of Prometheus, was made the first lasting attempt to organize education in the western world; here also was a university. It did not have the corporate name of "university"; and, reputedly, this gathering place of Greek scholars did not resemble the habitations of our present schools. But the spirit which pervades our modern institutions was there. This spirit which Greeks thought came down from heaven is forever modern, always new, but never changing.

Mythology teaches that it was Prometheus who gave men fire and that by this deed the wrath of the gods was aroused. Zeus in his anger ordained that the beneficent titan be chained to a rock where a vulture fed daily upon his liver, which grew whole again each night. The Greeks liked to compare fire to the restless intellect of man, and chains have long stood as the symbol of oppressed freedom. Chiron made his noble sacrifice and Hercules killed the vulture, and Prometheus was unbound. Can a university be put in chains? No, we can conceive the will and idea of a university as Promethean; it is the thing in man that despises chains. The Promethean spirit within a university demands that Truth, unadorned and unalloyed is the first business of the university. Where the Promethean spirit lives there exists a university. In modern times the university often becomes bound in links of artifice and irrelevance. There are many vultures which daily tear at its vital parts. But the parts keep healing, and soon there comes a Chiron and a Hercules, and the Promethean spirit is once again unbound.

OBJECTIFICATION AND INCORPORATION OF UNIVERSITAS.

There was a university in Ionia where the great Thales bade his students to look at the stuff of the world to find first principles. There was a university in southern Italy where Pythagoras led men in thought about the transmigration of the soul. Protagoras, the greatest of the sophists helped make all of Greece a university. Perhaps this pagan university had its greatest moment when Socrates faced his Athenian judges and declared plainly and evenly that "an unexamined life is not worth living."

The great schools of Zeno, Aristippus, Antisthenes, and Epicurus kept philosophy alive and growing. Later more men came to establish other schools, but most of them copied only the form, and seldom if ever did the spirit dwell within them. Even though the Promethean spirit had few places in which to live, its ethereal essence went on ministering to the hearts and minds of men the ennobling grace of wisdom. Where was the university of pagan Rome? In the days of the Caesars, Augustus and Tiberius, there was, in Judea, a Jewish carpenter who followed in the wake of John The Baptist. The carpenter was crucified, but not before he left his Truth as an inspiration for others, many others. Later there was Plotinus, Porphyry, Boethius, and Augustine. They are names, but they are names which we know because they personify the human passion for light and understanding; they exemplify the sovereign urgency to know. The university of those times was in farms and fields, mines and shops, temples and tents, and wherever else men sensed the idea of Truth and sustained the will to seek it.

But where does the critical historian seek the origin of a university? He searches the annals of men for signs of a corporation. Prior to the Middle Ages there were few. During the Middle Ages there were almost none. Plato's Academy survived more than eight hundred years. It was finally closed by Justinian in 526 A.D., The University of Paris was given a corporate charter in the year 1200. Some assert, therefore, that for 674 years there was no university, and, indeed, no higher education in the western world. By the standards of corporate existence this may be so. It is good that critical historians speak this way because by painstaking labor they give us bench marks, descriptions, and precise dates. But the closing of the Academy was nothing more than an eviction notice, and the Charter of the University of Paris was only a memorandum. The spirit of the university shifted its locale, entered into lively and more robust surroundings, and when corporate centers of learning became re-established in Western Europe, the men of scholarship were a hardy, fighting breed. During that long interval something had been added. Western scholars of the medieval university were relearning Aristotle in philosophy, but they had turned Socratic in matters of academic temperament.

The spirit of university was active and moving in this 674-year interval, but its travels are difficult to follow. Traces of it were discovered to have been at Salerno where learned men and scholars met to study medicine. It is said that Justinian himself established a school of law. Later the school seems to have transferred to Ravenna. By the eleventh century the school of law came to be recognized in the form of teacher and student guilds at Bologna. In the twelfth century this *studium* at Bologna was recognized by the corporate designation *universitas*. The spirit was also alive in France. What else could have emboldened the eleventh century monks of Beck to demand of Anselm, their abbot, an ontological proof of the existence of God? That great man, after acknowledging the primacy of his faith, gave it to them.

But the great celebrity in whom the Promethean spirit was most fully incarnated was the Parisian scholar, Abelard. One can feel reasonably assured that prior to the tenth century speculative philosophy and criticism did not exist in European institutions of education. Even the great Charlemagne, founder of the Palatine schools and himself a noteworthy scholar, was contented mainly with the study of grammars. However, by the eleventh century cities were forming, trade guilds had been established, and commerce flowered in the wake of the crusades. Men were on the move; Christendom had emerged as a supernational agency, and contact with civilizations of the East was growing. Conquests by the Franks and the Normans had spread the French language with its powerful philosophic idiom in all directions. Gradually, inexorably, Parisian France became the intellectual center of the world, the capital of human thought. Late in the eleventh century this handsome young man of twenty came to study at the Cathedral School of William of Champeaux. He was gay, amiable, talented, and of noble family. His name was Abelard.

No other man better personifies the mighty stirring of the human spirit which marked the twelfth century. His erudition was extraordinary for a man of these times. He wrote with great power in the vernacular, but knew Greek and Latin as well. Prior to his studies at Notre Dame, Abelard fatefully encountered the nominalism of Roscellinus. Thus, infected by an urgency to disputation, Abelard quickly challenged William, puzzled him, and finally silenced him. He immediately acquired a large following of students, and when the authorities failed to recognize his supremacy by installing him as a master of theology in the Cathedral School, he departed the city and established his mastership at Melun.

However, he soon returned to Paris and established his chair within the precincts of St. Genevieve, on the south bank of the Seine. His fame as a teacher continued to spread; he continued to study; and, at last, Abelard, by popular demand, was permitted to lecture as a master of theology in the Schools of Notre Dame. Thousands from all parts of Italy, Germany, France, and England came to hear him. The testimony on his oratorical powers is unanimous. A vision of this tall, graceful figure standing in masters' robes with hundreds seated about him in the straw has inspired more than one great artist. No one, it is said, reasoned more subtly than Abelard or handled the dialectical tool with more address. The ardor and intensity of his life, the charm and grace of his person are revealed in the letters of his unfortunate Heloise who loved him with an "immoderate love" and remained faithful until both their lives ended.

The details of his personal tragedy and undeserved persecution are recorded in many accounts of human infamy and need not be related here. They add poignancy to the romance of the university and detract nothing from the greatness of Abelard. He was a human voice, a voice which simplified, explained, dispelled theological obscurities, and made all smooth and easy. It is said that he reduced religion to philosophy and morality to humanity. A tradition holds that 20 of his students became cardinals and more than 50 became bishops. His writings were models of clarity. A brilliant logician, he raised questions, demanded answers. Prior to Abelard, the teaching license (*docendi*) was authorized by civil or ecclesiastical authority. After Abelard, the masters themselves demanded the privilege of issuing the license to teach, and nothing again was ever the same. When the masters declared that they and they alone should govern admissions to their guild, the modern university began its life.

Earlier it was stated that the Charter of the University of Paris was merely a memorandum. Prior to the Charter the masters and student guilds of Paris fought for the survival and the status of their membership. When moved to defense they would battle, when oppressed or overcome they would cease teaching, and when persecuted they would disperse. Cessation and dispersion were powerful economic weapons. It was an early Parisian dispersion which led to the founding of the University at Oxford. That town, once a prosperous market center, soon became as other university cities, a locus of boarding houses, inns, and eating places. The hint of dispersion in a university town was a threat of ruin to many townsmen. Accordingly, memoranda on the rights of scholars were issued from time to time. The Charter of the University of Paris issued by Phillip Augustus was issued in the face of dispersion. In effect, it was a recognition of the guild of masters, and an assurance of the masters' right to conduct the examinations for degrees. This Charter was not called an armistice, but it was drawn to that effect. Thus, at last, there came to be at Paris an institution with the corporate designation, *universitas*, and the spirit of the university was there.

The peace at Paris was short-lived; within 10 years new issues arose, and the masters were again embattled. This time the struggle centered upon an attempt by theologians to forbid the use of Aristotle's books on nature. Again, the masters won the freedom they believed necessary for the pursuit of Truth. The masters examined and controlled themselves. Therefore, they asserted no external control was wanted, needed, or justified. This victory has turned out to be a matter of immense importance. It stands as the primary basis of academic freedom. Having assured all the world that the spirit of criticism lived and that disputation was a constant responsibility of the corporation, the schoolmen claimed the right to speak and teach with impunity.

Thus, in the twelfth century an organized body of scholars existed, and the world around them found it necessary to grant them the rights to give their own degrees and to teach with freedom. The academic profession emerged, therefore, the sole judge of its own competence. In addition to these academic rights were other rights of lesser standing. These were specific to time and circumstances and applied to particular universities in particular cities. An example was the right of the university community to try to punish its own members for certain offenses, or the privilege of scholars and teachers to be tried and judged in ecclesiastical rather than secular courts. Another warranty was the right of travel. A recognized medieval scholar was a citizen of the world, and should he be possessed of the *jus ubique docendi* (a near universal teaching license), he was accorded the privilege of teaching in nearly any school.

All of these rights needed preservation, extension, and interpretation. If the community of scholars was to give its own degrees, procedures must then be established for examining, approving, and incepting the new masters. The freedoms of the community to decide on academic matters necessitated bylaws for decision making and implementation. The special nature of the relationship within the community itself and to the world without required a spokesman of some kind. Charters of privileges were granted by church and state, but negotiations with church and state remained a constant problem. These matters became the *functions* of the university corporation.

Having acquired definite functions, the university became an object in itself. As an object it was something more than a place to which men came to search for Truth. It became more than simply a recognized place where the quest for Truth itself is sovereign to all other concerns. But because the university was *incorporated* and *objectified* does not mean its autonomous *ideal* was necessarily altered or diminished. Without the *ideal*, nothing of the functions of the university made sense. The rules of chivalry which governed the inception of masters; the rules on making and selling books; the rules on lectures, fees, and examination were all charades without the *ideal.* It was the ideal which gave coherence and solidity to the functions. One who did not relate to the ideal simply did not understand the functions of the medieval university, as *today* many, not understanding the ideal, fail fully to understand the functions of a modern university.

THE PURPOSES AND PROCESSES OF ACADEMIC ADMINISTRATION. Again, therefore, we must declare that the university is an incarnation of the indomitable impulse to know. This impulse is expressed and felt by each man, but it is a property of mankind. Whenever and wherever this impulse is objectified and men can say, "Here, in this place dwells the Promethean spirit," there is a university. This spirit does not change. It is modern, always new. Some men say that change is constant and ubiquitous, what is modern today will tomorrow be obsolete. The spirit of the university is forever modern. It was modern to the pagan academy, modern to the medieval university, modern to the renaissance, and it is modern today. No matter how the objective aspects of a university change, the living spirit which dwells within does not change. It is the same, and it gives the university its essential nature.

As the thirteenth century ran its course, the functions of *universitas* made inevitable the tasks of *administration.* There are those who have made serious studies of the administration of medieval universities. There would be great profit in even more study of this kind. The academic men of today who administer schools should know more of their institutional ancestors. The medieval communities of scholars were the first which tried to preserve the ideal of the university while at the same time establishing machinery to effectuate its administrative functions. It was no easier then than now. The community of scholars soon succumbed to the acquisition of property, construction of buildings, and organization of libraries. As one might expect, it was not long before men mistook facilities for the university itself. If we asked them, where is the university, they would point to buildings.

In addition, the students were organized. In some communities it is said that student guilds predated the masters guilds. There were from the first numerous contests between students and masters, and students and the townsmen. Organized at first out of the necessity for their own protection, the time came to pass when student guilds oppressed individual scholars or masters and embraced privileges which were not relevant to either the ideal or the functions of the community. The difference between master, students, and townsmen had to be negotiated for the common good. Academic administration arose out of the sheer necessities of executing the functions of the corporation, preserving and improving its attributes, coordinating its various subgroups, and dealing with the universe of concerned laymen. Clearly the work of administration has been and is to align the dynamic elements of the university with the authentic ideal of a university.

The word *alignment* refers to that which distinguishes between the rectors, chancellors, provosts, deans, clerks, presidents, and proctors who succeeded and those who failed. Failures were many; they are designated in history by episodes of riot, anarchy, tyranny, lethargy, or excessive dominance by external patrons. Since the medieval times, the administrative tasks of a great university have been as sensitive and demanding as any in the institutional order. The administrator, regardless of his title, must first be a great teacher, a teacher who can communicate widely and effectively the university spirit to all who are within the community of scholars. He must, himself, understand the will and idea of the university, and he must be able to convince those who think of a university as buildings, people, finances, regulations that it is a great deal more than any or all of these things.

There are some today who exalt in the romance of the medieval university. They seem convinced it was a self-governing community which somehow kept itself in balance and alignment without anyone's holding serious responsibility or strong authority. Certain that this was the true state of affairs, the romanticists argue that academic administration should be little more than clerical work. Accordingly, the demand is often voiced that conventional administrative functions be dissolved into a faculty polylogue and that such executive functions as remain be given over to clerks. Such proposals have wide appeal in institutions which now function through an immense bureaucracy populated by arrogant and self-seeking administrators who seldom, if ever, have a human contact with students or faculty. Indeed, some men do serve selfish ends, but this derogates them and those who suffer them, not the task of administration. Plato was an academic administrator and so was Aristotle. The creative administrative talents of Robert Sorbonne led to the establishment of a school for Masters of Arts who wished to study for the Doctorate of Theology. This led to one of the great early reforms of western universities. Administration was not the primary profession of such men, but they or someone like them had to propose arrangements, enforce policies, and turn the attention of the community in this or that direction.

Regardless of how one feels about the prominence or visibility of administrative leaders in the academic community, he cannot mount a responsible approach to the functions of a university by simply devaluing administration. Certainly, there should be no more administration than needed to perform the necessary functions of the community. On the other hand, there should be no less than is necessary. Logic demands that such administration as a university requires should not be hobbled or frustrated by stratocratic committeedom. Though our valuation of the pristine immunities of the academic master continues high, the utility of the pristine conventions associated with those immunities is, in modern times, dubious. Often the critic of the modern university mistakes the convention for the value, and often modern faculties remember only the conventions and forget the values. If the faculty were to deliberate and act upon every matter of university business, faculties would be required to meet in continuous session. Obviously this cannot be the answer.

THE PROMISE OF AMERICAN UNIVERSITIES. A modern university lives in a modern city and not in a medieval city. Although the spirit of the medieval university is identical to the modern, the functions have modified, the corporate nature has changed, and the problems of governance and support are vastly altered. As much as some may wish to turn back the clock, it cannot happen. The medieval community of scholars is gone. There is nothing at all like it in the modern world. In North America the corporate form of the university is radically different from its medieval forbear. In Latin America and Europe some of the old forms are still visible, some of the old privileges still intact. But the students and professors of the continental university are not free. These universities are often dominated or used by political ideologists who are outside the community and have aims unrelated to the university.

Probably the most conspicuous distinction of the North American university is the fact that the North American model is not incorporated by the masters; and, in most cases, it is not incorporated for the masters. The incorporators of American universities usually have their principal interests outside of the academic profession and frequently view the university as instrumental to these interests. The American university has also been strongly influenced by the German ideals of scholarship and teaching. Specialized research is given a very high station on the hierarchy of academic values, and the scholar has a loyalty to his discipline which commonly overshadows his loyalty to the general community of scholars. The American university exists in a *milieu* wherein knowledge dissemination and knowledge making are regarded as essential. Thus, the modern American university is expensive. The medieval university could operate for nearly a century on the budget which supports the annual expenditures of any one of our medium-large American universities.

On the other hand, the American university, like the medieval university, has a vocational orientation. It is reasonably clear that the corporate form of the medieval university was strongly influenced by the function of admitting young men to the professions of medicine, law, clergy, and teaching. The American university is likewise a gateway to the professional world. As new professions came to exist, the American university has been quick to add training programs. The Continental and Latin American institutions, on the other hand, have not been quick to adapt to the vocational needs or aspirations of students. Thus, while maintaining great prestige they have drifted further from the realities of the civilization which supports their existence or mandates their functions.

Regional accreditation among the American schools, colleges, and universities is a characteristic which coheres with the best of the pristine traditions of the community of scholars. Regional accrediting bodies are actually organizations of corporations; in a sense they form a supercorporation. However, in performance they operate as a vast community of scholars. Their functions are to evaluate institutions—the institutions which compose their own membership—and, by awarding the accolade of accreditation, to assure the public and the profession that the institution is what it represents itself to be. Through accreditation, American scholars examine themselves and their own institutions.

In recent years American professions have organized their own special accrediting bodies. These, however, do not have the same alliance with the spirit of the university. Accreditors of professional programs speak directly of the quality of a specific public service which the university renders by a training program in medicine, law, education, or engineering. In the contradictions of regional and special accreditation is found a renewal of the same issues which brought the thirteenth century Parisian Masters of Arts into confrontation with Doctors of Theology. Again, these struggles are forever new, but they are more in the style of the American university than any other.

The paradox of university strife in both the old and new world is dramatized by the concern of the continental student, on the one hand, that his education is not vocationally useful, and the concern of the North American student, on the other hand, that his curriculum is shaped by the business and industrial needs of his society. It is against this unlike background that the time-honored struggle of the students and masters for autonomy in university matters is being waged in both worlds. The American model of the university increasingly demands that college administration raise vast sums of money to nourish an increasingly voracious community of scholars. Because so much money is needed, the successful money raiser falls heir to great power and prestige. In the characteristic old-world university the supremacy of the senior professors is sustained with a nominal level of support from government, student fees, and a few private sources. The European university is not so expensive.

One could well suppose, therefore, that the Promethean spirit would be more content in the old-world universities than in American institutions. However, the profanation and abuse of the ideal of the university can occur under a variety of circumstances. One of them, of course, is to have a squirarchy of senior professors and another is to have a hegemony of political figures who have professorial standing in the university community. The former is a pedagogical burlesque of the Order of Knighthood and contains its own Quixotic declensions, and the latter perverts the university, making it mistress to partisan political interests. Both of these circumstances are vividly present in old-world universities, and both frustrate and embarrass the ideal of the university. Prometheus is no more comfortable in the despotisms of European and Latin American institutions than in the administrative-minded, bureau-ridden North American models.

Administrative bureaucracy, therefore, does not represent the only form that an *establishment* might take. American universities may be too administration-minded, but one can argue with equal strength that old-world institutions are burdened with excesses which also vex the spirit of university. Among other things, this suggests that there is not a universal prescription for all universities to use in realigning themselves with their authentic ideal. All of them are displaced in different ways and each must seek within its own councils to examine itself and find its own way to authenticity.

Obviously, the American university must take a hard look at such things as the dominance of system in its educational style, the tendencies toward entrepreneurship in service and research functions, and the extraordinary outlays it must now put out for facilities. All of these things combine in ways which require the institution frequently to "hock its soul" in order to balance the budget. In effect, the academic profession should ask itself if it is necessary to continue the "by the numbers" style of undergraduate education which invites matriculants to have a go at *bucking the system through*. It should ask the *real price* the institutions pay for grant swinging, and it should wonder aloud if nonprofit corporations or government agencies might erect and maintain some of the expensively built and maintained laboratories and libraries. The university ought to be relieved of these burdens. Possibly steps such as these would enable the scholars to adopt modes of self-governance which are more consistent with the unadorned search for truth and with the sovereign mission of making more of their kind.

MODELS OF INTEGRITY. This is important not only for the American universities themselves, but also for the entire order of American educational institutions. The elementary schools, secondary schools, colleges, and governmental offices of education imitate university style in academic and administrative matters, and university values have a way of becoming pervasive of the entire institutional order. The current trading in academic credit by which course credit is converted to salary increments for teachers is a tragic example of this. Only the university can set such matters aright. Organizations of teachers must feel justified in proposals to barter credits for salary so long as the academic profession within the university makes no protest. Many local school boards agree, with great reluctance, to adopt other insensate forms of social or academic nonsense when it is established that the proposed fatuity exists in one or another university.

American universities have many trials before them. The great need is for creative administrative leaders who are sensitive to the authentic mission of the university in human affairs and have the capacity to lead faculties in thought and action toward this end. If these young American institutions, so full of potence and promise, become the preserve of Truth—the Truth that is for its own and no other sake—one way to broader reforms in all American schools will be manifest. In this, the responsibility of the university is clear. Without substantial reform at the university level, reform at any other level is difficult indeed.

But one feels it possible, in moments of meditation, when crossing the grounds and walking the halls of a great university. It is felt in the suspiration which is caused by nothing less than a direct sense of that divine spirit which came to man in that instant in which he became man. It is the spirit which keeps men driving, questioning, doubting, inquiring, probing; and it never rests. This restless essence dwells in the deep base of the university but shows itself in many ways, in the ardent flush upon the countenance of a young graduate student on his own for the first time in research, in the agitated voice of an undergraduate who first discovers professors do not agree, in the anticipation which hangs in the air prior to a great campus event, in the mien of students and teachers moving to and fro obviously simmering, obviously excited by ideas. One who looks upon and sees these things is seeing the real university. And one who sees the university in this way knows that it is possible to make the world understand that this is as much of the real idea of education as any mortal can perceive; the university has its great days, when these things are in full flower. In such times the season of hope is at its peak.

Those who administer must realize that they are forever one with those who teach and study in a community of scholars and that those who study and teach are forever one with those who administer. When all in the university community are at one with the will and idea of university, then the obscene and destructive struggles for power subside into disputation and discovery, teaching and examination, the first duties of the academic profession. Thus reformed, the American university can become the open source of integrity for all of American education, from nursery to graduate school. In truth, the most noble office which a university can perform is to discover and be itself.

But what a clarity of vision and a strength of purpose this requires! Vision and purpose are properties of men and not of their processes. Vision and purpose have existence in human wisdom and choice. No infusion of money can bring them on. The will and idea which dwells deep within a university was implanted long before men knew of dollars and will be there long after the last dollar has vanished. The essence of university is of an order which stands apart from the stream of temporal affairs, but those affairs can be greatly enriched by association with it. The clarity of vision and strength of purpose to accomplish this must be in those who lead and hold responsibility in the community of scholars. The Promethean spirit will be discontent until such men come forward and do their work.

ON FELICITOUS CHANGE

THE UBIQUITY OF CHANGE. When confronted with any demand for change one immediately recalls the poetic utterances of Heraclitus, the sullen and discontented sage of Ephesus who once proclaimed, "You cannot step twice in the same river for other waters are ever flowing on to you." This small fragment of change theory has come to be one of antiquity's best known pronouncements. It suggests that the natural order of things is an endless transformation wherein all is in process of becoming something else. Evolution, revolution, and involution are everywhere and forever. Constancy in the world of things has no presence. All is welter, and nothing abides, nothing survives except the massive fact of change itself.

Heraclitus gave us indication that even life and death are simply names of processes. Waking and sleeping are the same; youth and age are the same, "for the latter change and are the former and the former change back to the latter." Although men may dream of permanence and invariance, there is no permanence; nothing stays. If a man must depend on something he must depend on process. Nothing else deserves the working faith of a rational man.

Thus when a schoolman is asked to produce change, he might well reply: "What help does change need from me?" He may well feel the sentiment expressed by an octogenarian who, it is said, spends his quiescent days sitting stiffly atop a bench in the town square. When approached with the comment, "Sir, you've seen a great many changes in your time," he snapped, "I have, and I've been against every damn one of them."

Is it not then absurd to imply that any man, or any human agency, can do anything but accept change. Is not man himself a product of countless mutations across thousands of centuries? Did he not himself move upward along numerous paths of change? Is not his own intelligence, his power to question and to know, something which change has rendered? Is not man himself, like all other species of the natural order, an involuntary project constantly worked upon by process? Indeed, his body is imprisoned in the flux of the world;

it is constantly modified; and each generation of man differs somewhat from its predecessor. The man of nature is destined to remain ever unfinished, and forever unfinished is the nature of man.

THE QUEST FOR PERMANENCE. But the implication that one must facilitate change is not absurd. On the contrary, it is full of meaning. This meaning is somewhat submerged and requires unearthing.

As surely as men can see the ongoing flux of nature, there is in them a craving for permanence. So men create domains of permanence and into them they crawl as if attempting to rest for a bit, seeking a relief from the steady transformation which surges about them and beats within them. How is it that men can create permanence when all is change?

They can do this because they are producers of ideas. Ideas have permanence. The general idea of a circle is precisely what it was to the geometers who sat before Plato. The idea of a right angle triangle has maintained a steady life and meaning for centuries. Aristotle found permanence in the natural principles which the universe seems to obey. Augustine was an idealist, Aquinas a materialist, but both found a permanence in God's dispositions toward the world. Kant sensed the steady presence of a moral force in men, and he was willing to depend on it. Hegel depicted an absolute mind. Some modern existentialists see ever-present doubt and necessity of choice.

Once an idea is abstracted, locked into precise symbols, it can stand apart from the mad dance of time. Men of any age can recover it and have the experience of it. Ideas are given life by men, and some ideas have an immortality which lies beyond the reach of mere men. But although men can preserve ideas, the uses they make of them vary from time to time.

Therefore, contrary to the Platonic vision of abiding archetypes, the world of ideas often appears also to be a welter of forming, reforming, and changing notions. Why is this so? Although ideas themselves may have the quality of permanence, human credence changes. Men choose the ideas by which they will order and value their existence. Each new generation of men goes across the world of ideas and chooses anew. They never fail to choose some ideas their fathers chose; but they also never fail to vary. Thus 2600 years of western philosophy have not produced an undisputed metaphysics. We cannot anticipate anything different of the future.

Thus there are two changing orders: One is the natural order; the other is the ideological order. Men are joined to both of these orders, joined to the former by their bodies and joined to the latter by their thoughts. The natural order changes in obedience to standing natural principles. The physical world is never at rest. Its processes are inexorable, and the ways of matter can be foretold. But the ideological order is not so regular. There are seasons of new thought and new commitment. Perhaps the alternative periods of serenity and agitation in ideology reflect intervals when men have time to think; perhaps they reflect plateaus in man's enlightenment; or perhaps there is a wayward spirit which visits occasionally with the human race and stirs it with discontent. Whatever the source of this occasional perturbation, it is obvious that, today, great storms are tossing in the ideological domain and human credence is convulsed in a new season of choosing. In reference to it men speak of spirals or of pendulums, but these visitations of turbulence defy analogy to any object in the world of things.

The institutional order interacts with that of nature and of idea. If men live a civil life they must live by and in their institutions. Therefore, institutions must adjust to both the reality of nature and the reality of human credence. It is little wonder, therefore, that in the current season of turbulence in the ideological order institutional leaders are called upon to facilitate the change. But the leaders must understand that demands for change which stem from ideological turbulence are much more than the usual calls for perennial adjustment of institutional processes. This demand for change is a challenge to the very purposes of institutions. In such times institutional leaders must be prepared to sail on uncharted waters, and, today, schoolmen have this kind of adventure in prospect.

THE PROBLEM OF INSTITUTIONAL CHANGE. The public school is the principal educational component of the American institutional order. Both its utter magnitude and America's utter dependence upon it place singular burdens upon those who lead it. How will the present generation of schoolmen respond to the demand for change? One can be hopeful but not sanguine. If felicitous change is to be led by today's schoolmen, at least three problems must be overcome. The first two of the three seem not so great as the third.

The first problem is that the cadence of change in the ideological order is so rapid that we are required to accommodate revolution with machinery paced to evolution. Who could foresee two decades ago that the American school classroom would be selected as the major device for terminating racial segregation and all of its hideous consequences? The segregationist cry of *never* was answered by the integrationist cry of *now*. The answer of course came out to be *soon*, but soon did not mean a century; soon came to mean two generations. Who could foresee five decades ago that American homes, the American churches, and American philanthropies would, by yielding increasing measures of responsibility, create an institutional gap in the realm of religious values? Who would have imagined that the burdens of public service would be aggravated by a steadfast and growing belief that society must safeguard the physical welfare of each individual? The vexations these developments have produced in public education need no elaboration here.

The second difficulty is that those who direct the massive enterprise of public education have an undeniable bias which favors its past and present condition. The public school establishment has, after all, a vast mechanical component. It runs on policy and procedures. It is held together by those who have proven their ability to regulate it. Such men have been rewarded by it. They have been assigned to positions of distinction for which they stand justly proud. It must be expected, therefore, that a kind of animistic loyalty would exist in those who again and again have been accorded such accolades as the present complex of arrangements can present.

The author recalls his own enthrallment with the establishment on the day he was approached from on high and informed of his elevation to the principalship of a school. It was at that point that his own confidence in the insight and profound discernment of the system soared to greater heights. Why, he might well have then spoken, would an agency capable of such wisdom ever stand in need of significant change?

There is, as a consequence, human inertia to overcome, and this is joined by the mechanical inertia inevitable in such a massive enterprise which is required to interact with legislative activities and their companioning political realities. If these problems are met we are confronted by a portion of our great corps of specialists who are made obsolete by any significant change. To this is added the fact that the same change calls for a group of new specialists who are as yet untrained.

The third difficulty, and, in this view, the most serious of the three, is reflected in the style by which most practicing schoolmen have been trained for their work. *They are process men!* None of today's schoolmen were in on the era of vision during which the public schools were formed. All have been trained in a century when education turned toward the social sciences and our most distinguished scholars were students of social processes. Indeed, this scholarship has been of tremendous value. The new insights on the nature of society and the processes of change within the institutional order will serve the generations of schoolmen to come as well as the works of the great men of antiquity, the middle ages, and the renaissance have served the present. This century is honored because John Dewey was part of it.

But process is neither right-headed nor wrong-headed. It is no-headed. It is one thing to construct theoretical models on how Americans behave in a society. However, it is quite another thing to know how it feels to be alive in America, facing the problems, and feeling the aspirations, hope in heart, passion in stomach. For this we are quite naturally drawn to the humane or intuitive disciplines. These are the studies through which man looks inwardly at himself. These are the studies which furnish the *ought* of civilized life. Science does not take the inward path to truth. Social scientists, when true to the scientific tradition, look out upon the world to see what *is*. Their truth is in cognate facts. When social scientists confront the problems of *ought*, they must do so as *men*, and their science departs.

The point is that although modern school leaders have been well trained in social science and social process, they have not, for the most part, been strongly associated with the vision-producing elements of the modern ideological order; and, even worse, they have not effective communication with the artists, writers, and Utopians of our own time. Of course it will be asserted that poets can not run schools. But as an alternative to this, must we have a school administrator with no poetry in him?

Who were Plato, Aristotle, Quintilian, Pestalozzi, Froebel, Comenius, and Strum? What did they have in common? It was certainly not their philosophical methods. It was not their beliefs about education. *All of them headed schools.* Not all were successful as administrators; but were it not for their schools, it is quite likely we would know all of them less and know some of them not at all.

But this is an era when the men who operate schools are not at the head of the ideological order, nor are they in the middle. They are far back in the train, craning their necks to see what is going on ahead.

To paraphrase Hamlet, their consciousness of uncertainty makes them cowards, who rest secure in the processes studied so long that the native hue of resolution is sicklied over by the pale cast of committee deliberations or vanishes entirely through that magnificent escape hatch called the need for additional study. Of course, it is true that the nature of public school responsibility makes radicalism on the part of schoolmen impossible. But schoolmen can move up on the ideological train; they need not be so far back. We must remind ourselves that students of education ought to study purpose as well as process and that their responsibility to speculate is as great in one as in the other.

We can be grateful that American pragmatism has given us a real view of the *learner* and a concept of *society*. But it must be regretted that it has taken us away from a proper reflection upon *man* and *civilization*. We can appreciate certain insights into learning and teaching produced by the tightly reasoned methods of educational research. But these methods have come to lay a dead hand of pattern across our thought about what men and civilization can become. Without inspired visions of these, our will to action is dissolved by fear of action.

VISION AND LEADERSHIP. We do have a few visionaries about, but usually these have been imported from other fields. As such, their visions are crude and unnurtured by meaningful experience with the problems. From school leaders there are few thoughts produced except those of larger administrative arrangements (more dollars back of each child); federal or foundations dollars for innovators (well established scholars often defending forts); new dimensions in teacher education (each man shall do his duty to sustain classroom teaching); and more research which tells us that poor people fit a hypothesized concept of poor people, that deprived children conform to our description of deprived children, and that people who live in the center of a city are influenced by the environment which exists there. Then, too, there is a strangely ambitious group who want to nationalize or federalize standards, or processes, or financing. This simply assumes that there can be developed through the national community a wisdom about what education should be which is better than can be found by men in many communities, working near their homes in deliberation with their neighbors, watching the children they know grow, and enjoying the life-fulfilling experience of shaping something of their future. This, of course, is another argument.

Americans have a faith in schooling which is deep, implicit, and abiding. For many, it is their religion. Recently, a school board member, who was also a union leader, turned angrily upon the board's educational consultant and, pounding on the table, said, "You (sic) got to tell us how to make the schools better." Really, the whole country is pounding the table with this mandate. To change the metaphor, good schooling is a ladder to a superior station in life and everyone wants to go up.

Americans have been afflicted by Levana, the Roman goddess, who, it was said, brought men to know aspiration. This "office of ennobling kindness" is described by De Quincy in *Sighs from the Depths*.

> At the very moment of birth, just as the infant tasted for the first time the atmosphere of our troubled planet, it was laid on the ground . . . but, immediately, lest so grand a creature should grovel there for more than one instant, either the paternal hand, as proxy for the goddess Levana, or some near kinsman, as proxy for the father, raised it upright, bade it look as the king of all this world, and presented its forehead to the stars, saying, perhaps in his heart, behold what is greater than yourselves.

The spirit "Levana," who is everywhere in America, derived her name (according to De Quincy) from the Latin verb *levare* which means "to raise aloft." America's enchantment with Levana is by reason of selective breeding. For three centuries the oceans of this world bore a great assortment of passengers to this land, each of whom chose himself on the strength of an aspiration that he could be "greater than himself." For each it was an emboldened venture taken in the hardy resolve that his greatness could be known to himself and his progeny; many failed en route. The hardy and fortunate survivors shaped our American heritage, and we are their sons.

Levana is the pervasive motivity of the American people, but her challenge is no longer in the form of an ocean or an uncharted wilderness. It is schooling. Schooling is the way up, and everyone expects to go up. Time does not weaken the resolve nor temper the passion. American schoolmen must understand that the pleadings of such people can not go unheeded.

Any real expression of hope for felicitous change in American schooling must begin as an unabashed exhortation that schoolmen step forward and lead in accordance with the most renowned traditions of their profession. Emerson proclaimed, "There is properly no history, only biography." He wrote, "Civil history, natural history, the history of art and the history of literature must be explained from individual history, or must remain words." This is a nation which still reveres manhood. School leaders, hanging back in worried anticipation over what a faceless "they," are going to do, simply invite aggressive opportunists in publishing, testing, business, politics and other combinations to chart directions for public education. It is worse still that schoolmen are constantly in reaction, saying no to what others propose while America pounds the table seeking new vision for her schools.

It is regrettable that so many schoolmen are imbued with a philosophy which views only an indeterminate world of undestined process, which finds fundamental reality in socially experienceable processes, which tends to "humbug" the reality of mind, and which turns its back upon determinism through the interaction of nature, idea, and choice. What a poor view it is that presents man's physical and social processes as his major source of strength! What a poor view it is that leaves the question of "good" to the public taste! The unrest of our times reminds us that men still crave to order their lives upon chosen ideals. Should we embrace this view of man if we are to perform the office of ennobling vision for American education?

TOWARD THE HUMANITIES. In extending this theme, it has been suggested that there are many ways to kill a man. One, it can be supposed, is to prevent his coming alive. Children are more than mere social phenomena to be conditioned for the requirements of physical cooperation, interdependence, and, indeed, subservience which social reality places upon them. Educational theory wants more than the views propounded by biologists, psychologists, and the like. There is a selfhood for each child. The ideology of our times demands of education that each selfhood be actualized.

Thus, theories of "adjustment" and the rationale of "needs" are not enough to satisfy the yearnings of the emerging ideology. We can not satisfy our age with a vision of a constantly reconstructed social order. Today's mind wants to know how we are going to bring warmth, beauty, love, justice, and fulfillment into each of the separate and individual lives which find their presence in our civilization. Gone is the subject center; gone is the psychological center; gone is the social center. We are arrived at an era when education is not asked to solve the problems of industry, of government, of civil order. It is a positive vision—one born of inspiration, not desperation. Education is invited to give something to each man. We are to provide the support each man requires in his struggle for a life of meaning and satisfaction.

You can kill a man with schooling which is devoted entirely to what he can *do* and not at all to what he can *be*. Our schools smell of technology now, and yet there are those who wish to raise the levels of artifice even higher. Great agencies of mass communication have heralded a stream of proposals for national standards of cognate achievement. Such plans are offered in a favorable light which makes little mention of the invidious comparisons and inane values that are by-products of such enterprise. Nothing would more quickly complete the transformation of our beloved schools into pernicious instrumentalities for pummeling and punching young people into adult stereotypes possessed, in some measure, of a standard set of skills. Such noble and creative impulses as they may have would need to be hardy to survive such schooling. With this part of him dead, is it too much to say that we have killed a man?

Many children come home from modern schools with their competitive instincts honed to a sharp edge of bitterness. They quarrel at dinner and family evenings are marked by recrimination and rebuke. And why not? Is anyone in American education teaching them the fuller meanings of love? Humane teaching has not been in style!

So America goes on, pounding the table, calling out for quality in schooling. It is to the credit of the public that it has not been persuaded to agree that quality in education simply means accumulation of even more academic skills or the storing up of greater volumes of cognate knowledge. The people do not seem to approve of that view and are asking for another; moreover, they want their local schoolmen, whom they know, and usually like and trust, to produce it. So far only a few schoolmen have given such vision to the community they serve. How long will the public wait?

Felicitous change has occurred in the history of American education. It is recognized as occurring when the educational style of schools is adapted to correspond with the emerging ideological credence of the public. Horace Mann, Henry Bernard, and William Harris among others recognized the dreams on the nineteenth-century horizon and stepped forth with the richly imaginative conception of free public education, normal schools, and universal literacy. The felicitous change of today will be achieved by schoolmen who lead the way to individualization of classroom teaching and the humanization of school curricula.

But, one might ask—what of the heroes among us who are leading our schools in escalades upon the high walls of urban unrest, who maneuver school population areas to achieve a fuller racial mix, and who offer the ghetto child an exaggerated diet of skills? These are cruel proceedings; and, in and of themselves, are useless. Is a school a weapon to strike with? Are our schools ploys in a grand social design? We must recognize that the unrest, the racism, and the ghetto are vexations of the human spirit. The ghettos exist in American cities because millions of Americans nowhere near the city have ghettos in their hearts. So long as the ghettos are in human hearts they will be incarnated somewhere in the world of places and events. The same can be said of racism.

A good school is simply an environment in which men are altered in the direction of greatness. The best strategy to deploy against current and future problems is to create good schools, as many as possible, wherever possible. To do this schoolmen must be schoolmen and not social tacticians. Rather than a "great society" we must strive for a society of great men, each of whom have learned to reach toward the fullness of a personal truth. As this end is approached, the problems which so obsess our present times will become part of a vanishing American past.

Such felicitous change, however, demands that men of our times stand forth as did Bernard, Mann, Harris, and others. They must lead in the thinking of what great schools are in the rural areas, the suburbs, and the cities. By taking in their own hands the reins of change, they will direct the ride into the future. Even now there is a vision of a civilization which prizes scholars above soldiers, men of service above men of trade, men of thought above men of power. None are better situated to incarnate a vision of schooling which matches these values than those now in charge of American public schools. If the time comes when the present variety of schoolmen are asked to stand aside as others take control, it will not be said that they were denied their hour of opportunity.

MEDITATIONS FOR A BEGINNING TEACHER

ON THE MORAL FOUNDATIONS OF TEACHING. In regard to antiquity, the art of teaching is the rival of any. In diversity of precedent the profession of teaching equals any. Scribes and prophets, apostles and pedagogues, apprentice masters and priests, magicians and philosophers are each characteristic examples. In every society, those who teach have collective identity, distinctive responsibilities, and unique expectations. American professional teachers are no less concerned with these matters. One forthright protocol for their treatment is embodied in the ethical code of the National Education Association.

Ethical maxims are invariably drawn from a broader set of convictions which, in this case, could be called the moral foundations of teaching in the United States. Maxims have the purpose of regulating conduct, a clear necessity for any enterprise in which many are joined. However, it is vital that persons governed by any code reflect often upon its moral foundations. Otherwise its maxims are soon unappreciated, later despised, and ultimately unheeded. Obviously, this means that teachers must do a great deal of thinking about teaching.

Some teachers view teaching simply as a mission to perpetuate the knowledge and heritage of the society which employs them. Others may condemn this as simply assuring that the superstitions and prejudices of the past generation are enlarged and absorbed by the new. Still others, on the other hand, think of teaching as liberating the mind from the past, sending it winging in search of truth, and whatever other ends that may bring. These say with Socrates that the unexamined life is not worth living. But many of their colleagues respond by saying this kind of thing substitutes anarchy for order. It brings youth to riot and revolt and "makes strangers of the gods."

More recent thinkers offer a version that a teacher is a kind of broker between the child and his environment, helping the former to conceptualize the latter. A great many modern authorities agree with John Dewey that education has no external goal but is simply the reconstruction of experience. These teachers, they often say, teach children, not subjects. Some maintain the central point of their work is to safeguard the individual's freedom to exercise his potentials, this being the object of order and the highest good. Others are satisfied if children and youth "behave themselves" by conforming to the predetermined order of the classroom.

This is not an essay on the relative merits of these differing aims. Of interest here is the fact that teachers are not and never have been agreed on the values and ends of teaching. Therefore, it is clear that common ethical garments are worn by a wide range of fellows and factions at work in diversified institutions, believing many different things about school, civilization, and the purpose for order. It is natural that a young professional, in viewing such widespread unlikeness and dissimilitude, should wonder if American teachers have enough in common to establish a moral foundation for their work.

They do. The polylogue is continuous, concord is never achieved, and the dissonance is often painful. But there is a spiritual unity. Although there may be wide disagreement about the nature of man, American teachers hold in common a Promethian concern for his well being and a Promethian belief that learning presents man with greater dimensions for life and offers ampler possibilities for being. Despite their multiform theories on the origins of man's spirit of inquiry, and divided notions of how best to nourish it, American teachers are unmixed in their commitment to keep it aflame. They care very deeply about things bigger than themselves of which they are only part. Among them there is discord on the ends of social order, but there is accord on the need for improved order. There is discord on what institutions best serve the interests of man, but there is accord on the need for strong institutions. Teachers shape a great portion of the public conscience. Frequently they lead the way in applying that conscience to public questions. Even though, as in other matters, they disagree, their conversation helps lead the public to higher ground. In school they are components of an environment of ideas. Although American teachers hold no ideology in common, each constantly redevelops his own by bringing it to interaction with those developing around him. This is part of the academic life in which all teachers should join and which they should come to enjoy.

Finally, among professional teachers, there is universal reverence for the art of teaching. In recent times organizations of teachers have formed wherein reverence for teaching itself is small and ideological concerns do not exist. Such groups tend only to deal with the more limited problems of salary and benefits. The academic profession is quite naturally interested in salaries and benefits. The current pre-eminence of such considerations in the work of professional associations offers abundant evidence of this. But uppermost in the true professional is a reverence for the art of teaching, its beauties and potencies. No organization of professional teachers has an inherent claim on the loyalties of teachers, but the professional is most at home in a group whose moral concern for the state of the art most closely matches his own.

Thus, the first commandment for the new professional teacher is a prescription seldom given out in this age of quantification and instant response. He is asked to meditate. The quality of his thought about his art will quite probably be matched later by the quality of his contribution to it. If in his thinking he can discover, among other things, his own concern for man and for society, his own commitment to truth, his developing ideology, and his reverence for the art, he will begin to understand and appreciate the foundations of teaching in the United States. He will also be able to give fuller meaning to the ethical canons which enjoin all teachers at work.

ON SELECTING A POSITION. As one might expect, teachers who think about teaching have strong feelings about the circumstances under which they teach. However, school administrators of long experience have noted that during employment interviews inexperienced teachers are often content to discuss only salary and benefits. It seems that newcomers to the profession are more apt to select their position on the basis of a few dollars' difference in annual salary. Established teachers, on the other hand, tend to go much further in their analysis of a prospective position. They assign greater importance to finding the conditions under which they can do their best work.

The wisdom of this is so plain that it is difficult to understand why a more thorough analysis is not made by all who seek teaching positions. Certainly the teacher applicant and his prospective em-

ployer should exchange views on teaching. Disagreement between
the two is not necessarily fatal to the prospect of employment. Educational leaders recognize that wholesome dissent is of great value
in educational institutions. Good educational administrators accept
it; indeed, they cultivate a tolerance for dissent among the faculty.

All good teachers do not teach alike. If one finds authority
figures in an educational institution enforcing conformity with respect
to teaching methods, the probability is very strong that few good
teachers are there. On the other hand, any concentration of good
teachers will display a great variety of methods and techniques, each
teacher using that which is best in his own hands. This is as it
should be.

Descriptive materials are helpful in understanding a school, but
a school is, after all, an environment. If it is possible, one interested
in teaching in a school should visit a school while it is in operation.
Meeting the faculty, observing students at work, and looking in
upon such things as cafeteria operation, student assemblies, and school
dismissal offer tonal dimensions which are invaluable in making a
decision.

Finally, it must be emphasized that professional fulfillment is
available in many places, not just in the "well scrubbed" neighborhoods. Some of the best and most vital teaching in America is done
in population centers where few go to college. Many young teachers
want most to teach in the kind of school they attended. Certainly
this is understandable, but there are some very good reasons for
seeking a different environment in which to begin a teaching career.
One of the most important of these exists in the possibility that
under new circumstances increments of insight and growth will
probably be achieved. The professional beginning is a great adventure. It should offer the young teacher more than just the most
money he can get.

Those who guide young teachers, including parents, teacher
educators, and experienced colleagues, should not discourage the
enthusiasm of neophytes for taking on the overwhelming problems
of classroom teaching in the large urban centers. The hope which
education holds out to the children of the ghetto must be borne on
the enthusiasm of young people, who have yet to be convinced there
is anything they can not do. More than anything else the children of
the ghetto need inspiration. This quality comes forth only from the
young and the young in spirit.

ON PROFESSIONAL RIGHTS. The legal foundations of American education afford certain rights to teachers. These derived from older traditions which have been modified by the unique declensions of law and educational practice in America. It would violate the character of this essay to present a detailed listing of rights. However, four areas are important to consider: (1) the right to associate, (2) the right to authority, (3) the right to professional development, and (4) the right to tenure. Anyone connected with a school should be acquainted with teacher rights in these areas. They have been won and tested again and again during the 24 centuries of organized education in western civilization.

Many modern teachers regard the right to associate only as an opportunity to win increased personal benefits. A study of the history of teaching would soon reveal this view to be erroneous. Associations of teachers have been primary forces in developing institutions of learning into the civilizing agencies they are. The teachers' guilds comprised the first recognized form of the medieval university. Western education, as we know it, is the offspring of these groups.

There have been martyrs to academic freedom as long as there have been teachers. The right of teachers to associate in defense of academic freedom can be traced to events resulting from a ban on reading or lecturing on Aristotle's books on natural philosophy at the University of Paris early in the thirteenth century. In a dramatic exchange, the masters of arts established the lecture hall as a privileged domain for the pursuit of truth, even if such a pursuit would lead to doubts about established values. Subsequent tests of this right have made lively history, but this right has survived along with a responsibility which must be simultaneously applied. This responsibility is discussed later.

From English common law has derived a doctrine that, in the presence of the child, a teacher stands in the place of the parent. Thus, the general statement can be made that the authority of a teacher is that of a parent. But public school teachers are also employees of the state. The state is sovereign on most questions affecting educational practice in the United States. Therefore, the doctrine of parental authority can and has been modified by legislative and court action.

The result has been that some states have mitigated the rights of a teacher to use corporal punishment. Other states have not yet overthrown this ancient prerogative, but courts appear increasingly inclined to bring charges against teachers and bring teachers to trial who chastise students in this way. Many school boards have declared policies against corporal punishment, and there is a changing attitude in the public and in the profession on both the educational value and moral justification of corporal punishment. Evidence is mounting that a teacher's action on the person of a student is disapproved by students, parents, and the profession. Although this right, in this limited sense, remains in many states, the practicality of its exercise in an atmosphere of disapproval is highly dubious. Obviously, it belongs to an era that has passed. Authority rights pose complex and interesting academic questions. Good teachers know them, but seldom, if ever, invoke them. Good teaching is inspired, and inspiration carries a discipline of its own. Such teaching is based on rules which stand higher than those written by men.

An area of teacher rights which is receiving increasing attention is that of continuous professional development. Long observed in the scholarly climate of the great universities where frequent sabbaticals or leaves of absence are commonplace, the recognition of this right is now becoming much more general. Modern elementary and secondary teachers are expected to continue their self-development. However, the expectation is not, as yet, universal. Many teachers still are reluctant to make full use of sabbatical provisions, and some school directors receive such requests with enmity.

But it is unthinkable that a modern teacher should attempt to sustain full career without periodic renewal or redevelopment! As evidence of the growing acceptance of this need, there are many agencies creating opportunities for in-service teachers to engage in part-time or full-time study. Each year more teachers are freed to engage in study or travel. Full consummation of a professional career requires self-development. Modern teachers have this right.

Public education in the United States began with schools operated by the neighborhood. Some of the boards of control were elected, others appointed. The public school developed under the leadership of community laymen. However, when school systems began the professionalization of teaching and administration, serious problems arose—not the least of which was the occasional unsavory political activity in connection with the employment of teachers. Partly as a consequence of this, the policy of professional tenure became established in American public schools.

Professional tenure, however, is not new. It is a long-established custom in distinguished institutions. The conditions under which it is achieved and maintained vary from place to place. All tenure plans have the purpose of eliminating the capricious hiring and dismissal of teachers. Most states have instituted legal provisions respecting the tenure of public school teachers. It is recognized that without some form of tenure agreement, teaching of any kind is very difficult. A reputable school, therefore, will not be without a tenure plan for teachers.

A teacher is a teacher all the time, but the range of personal activities open to him must certainly be as great as that open to any creditable citizen. His freedom to be active in the civic life of his community, to speak on public issues, to vote, and to give open support to political candidates is limited only by his obligation not to associate his school or his profession with his private views. In addition, he must be in a position to resist undesirable infringement on the school by others who wish to invoke the name of the school or the profession in behalf of a personal cause.

Tenure makes these things possible. It is a hard-won right which enables the modern teacher to achieve dignity in his personal life and to teach truth with impunity. Each generation of teachers is obliged to defend it. The defense is conducted from two positions: the first is represented in a profession fully knowledgeable of the meaning and importance of tenure; the second is represented in a profession which jealously guards against its abuse by its own members. Properly used and regarded, the tenure of teachers is a benefit to civilization.

ON PROFESSIONAL RESPONSIBILITIES. If there is a central theme to any essay on beginning teaching, the theme must include the idea of responsibility. Discourse on the professional responsibility of teachers is often solemn and may become downright melancholy. The impression grows that teaching is heavy-hearted work best managed by the grim and grave. Of course every teacher should include at least one soaking wet blanket in his "kit of tools." There are times when his charges will display more gusto than anyone can possibly use. But teachers are not a somber lot. In fact, successful teachers are more often infected by cheerfulness. Although no one can be certain, they probably teach as well as they do because their approach to the task is with an unvexed spirit. The work is serious, but it is not deadly.

It is logical that a specific discussion on the rights of a professional teacher would be followed by an analysis of his responsibilities. It is impossible to know if right or responsibility is inevitably followed by a withdrawal of right. This is what teachers teach their students, and it is what their profession teaches them. Thus the theme of responsibility rises to crescendo on every occasion when teachers invoke their rights.

Teachers have a right to associate but they must associate responsibly. The thirteenth century masters at the University of Paris proclaimed the right of academic freedom with the declaration that the academic profession examines itself and therefore needs no external control. Thus, academic freedom was born to teachers on the strength of their declaration to their own responsibility.

This presents something of a modern issue. If we accept the idea that freedom of this kind belongs only to a group of teachers who accept the responsibility for rigorous self examination, why is it that those critics of elementary and secondary education who enjoy the greatest public credibility are persons with little or no experience in that part of the teaching profession? The question seems to arise: have elementary and secondary teachers been sufficiently vigorous in criticizing themselves? Can it be that by failure of vigorous self-examination the right of professional self-determination might soon be forfeited entirely? Young professional teachers should ponder this.

The same is true of any other aspect of the right to associate. The teacher "strike" is a controversial point. A day of school lost to children is forever lost. There is no way for a student to retrieve it. In addition, the sensitive balance of an educational institution is difficult to restore when upset by teachers who take their disputes before the students and the public. There is a strong difference between dialogue on scholarly issues and rancor over working conditions. Bitter and undignified conduct by teachers is harmful to those who are in school at the time. The question is not whether teachers have a right to strike. The masters at Paris not only ceased, they also dispersed. But their students were able to follow them. The question is: what responsibility do teachers feel toward those who are in their classrooms? In a modern strike by classroom teachers, the organized program of education ceases, and each day of school lost is lost forever.

There is a decisive difference between an industrial plant and a school. An assembly line can be stopped; students do not stop.

Thousands of homes in every community depend on the fact that school will open when scheduled. Motors are indifferent to what goes on; students are not; they have deep feelings about their teachers, and they get involved. A factory can be restored to normal operation in a few minutes. A school takes many days. So the answer is that responsible teachers do not strike.

This does not mean that associations of teachers must simply forbear such unsavory conditions as may be present in their school. It does mean that they should correct deficiencies without disrupting the education of students. Such a sense of responsibility is not known so much as it is felt; it does not have a specific time and place. It is pervasive. As teachers face authority problems, in-service education problems, and tenure problems, they maintain their personal decorum and their professed fealty to the educational welfare of the students. This is one of the hallmarks of the profession and one of the very good reasons for being part of it. There are some who will not understand what this means, and this is a very good reason why these persons should consider some other kind of work.

Teachers have responsibilities as individuals as well as the responsibility they exercise in association with other teachers. Most of these come to light in professional training. However, circumstances vary with each position. Again the matter of attitude stands colossal. "Craftsmanship" is an old-fashioned word which, lamentably, is seldom used in modern times. A professional teacher, in a sense, is a craftsman with a craftsman's pride in his performance. He makes a strong point of knowing his duties thoroughly and executes them in a befitting manner. His work has no unimportant aspect.

The amalgam of faculty operation is the sum of individual performances. Therefore, the responsibility to be at the station of duty, at the correct time, fully prepared, equals in every respect the obligations to prepare a curriculum, teach classes, evaluate students, report their progress, and, at all times, attend to their health and safety. These individual transactions are conducted with the consciousness that they contribute as well to the achievement of a group.

The professional also marks those responsibilities which are collateral to teaching. These include performing the obligations associated with community relations, developing his own interest in the extra class activities, and counseling students where appropriate. A teacher is a teacher to the students, even when not in school. Those who wish the identification to drop as they leave the building will be disappointed. Again, those who can not bear to be professional teachers, at all times, with all that it implies, had better find something else to do.

ON PROFESSIONAL CONTRACTS. That which works well is seldom discussed. This is true of the system of teacher contracts currently used in educational practice. It works well for two reasons: one is that nearly everyone respects it; the other is that almost everyone is prepared to be reasonable on the few occasions when one or both parties find it difficult to fulfill the terms. With rare exceptions these agreements are made in good faith, and it would be difficult to find a covenant in either the business or the professional world that is more faithfully kept.

One occasionally hears that a teacher is holding two contracts during a period of indecision. It is good that this happens so rarely. Double contracting is on a moral par with bigamy. Two schools are under the impression they have a teacher. One of them does not, and that school is turning away qualified candidates while the philandering teacher makes up his mind. If a young teacher is not certain he wants the position, he must not sign the contract. If he does sign the contract, he must keep it.

The teacher contract is a relatively simple document. Usually, there are two kinds: one is for the beginning teacher who is "a temporary professional employee," so called because he has not achieved tenure status, and the other is for the "permanent professional employee" who has earned tenure. The contract document usually contains no variables other than the salary, dates of employment, title, and special provisions.

Many things are part of the contract which are not specifically written on the document—for example, the rules and regulations of the board of education (or board of control or corporation in the case of private schools). The document may also refer to the laws of the state, thus making those laws part of the agreement without quoting them directly. The teacher's schedule which comes with the authority of the board of education then becomes a part of the contract *per se*.

The contract, therefore, includes a great deal more than salary, dates, and title. When the teacher signs the contract he is agreeing to a great variety of conditions which he learned about when he appeared for his interview. But there is invariably a host of things which can not be learned in this way or, for that matter, any other way short of working in the school. So most teachers rely heavily on the reputation of the school and act in good faith. On the other side, neither does the school know everything. The contract in this larger sense becomes an expression of the faith each of the parties holds in the other; and as indicated earlier, it works very well. This is both to the credit and to the gratification of members of the teaching profession.

Because it works well both the school and teacher can deal in certainty with one another after the contract is made. Obviously, this has a favorable effect upon the teaching that is done. Both school and teacher, each confident of the other's integrity, can move directly on the problems of education. The new professional teacher, therefore, inherits an honorable and valuable tradition. He is expected to maintain this tradition in his own professional conduct.

Finally, if extreme circumstances arise, and a teacher finds it necessary or vitally important to request release from his contract, the odds are very good that the request will be given every consideration. School administrators dislike placing the advancement of anyone on their present staff under delay or jeopardy. Contrary to what is often claimed, largeness of spirit is a common quality in school administrators. Often they have been known to abbreviate summer vacations or go to even greater extremes in order to be helpful. This, too, is a product of the fine tradition of sincerity and good faith which stands back of professional contracts. However, if the adjustment can not be made to the satisfaction of the school, the teacher should then perform according to his contract. It is the way of the profession—and a very good way, as events have proved.

ON PROFESSIONAL DEVELOPMENT. In-service *growth* is a professional parlance which the new teacher quickly learns to use in conversation. It is interesting that we can reduce changes in so fine and mysterious a thing as the human personality to such a simple word as *growth*. Any essay on this subject could move in many directions, such as personal maturity, keeping up-to-date, acquiring higher academic distinctions, and extensive travel. So the user of the word growth means what he chooses it to mean. In reality, one can suppose, it can mean all of these things.

The commitment to growth can be described as meaning the teacher will use every means available to become a better teacher.

Each member of the profession has his own artistic potential. Morality in art is a complicated thing, but there is almost universal agreement that the artist has a moral obligation to become as good as he can. This, of course, means something different for each.

The problem has been with us for a very long time. But it is only recently that the academic profession attempted to deal with it in a systematic way. In retrospect, much fault can be found with the first efforts, and the profession will be long at work to find its way out of the difficulties which were caused.

For one reason or another the earliest solutions to the problem tended to prescribe much of the in-service development of teachers. Some will say that it is now badly overprescribed. Critics point with despair to policies which convert graduate or postbaccalaureate credit into a new "species of the realm." Many school boards are implementing programs which offer automatic salary increases as a reward for acquiring additional credit. One of the few unbecoming spectacles in the teaching profession is seen in the cynical teacher who enrolls in a graduate course simply to earn credits for a salary increase. Only slight redemption is gained from the fact that many teachers achieve some growth from this reluctant exposure.

On the other side, the economic realities of the day present very convincing reasons for acquiring additional credit for additional salary. Proponents of the policy argue that participating teachers show some effort at growth, they acquire some useful experiences, and increased salaries are in the common good. The algebraic sum, they say, is on the plus side, and, indeed, this may well be.

But the new professional teacher is left with a number of problems. The first, as was said, is the moral problem of how to grow. Is further study the way to professional growth? If it is, then the question becomes: what kind of study? Broadly there are two: the first is continuing undergraduate study. This can be either in the professional area on the academic specialty, or in general education. The second is in graduate study. This differs from undergraduate study in that it has a research component, it is internally directed, it often requires a period of residence in an academic community, and is done in an environment especially equipped for the purpose.

Possibly the way to professional growth is not through additional study. Unfortunately, schools have not found a widely accepted means for implementing other ideas. It is difficult to find increments of growth which rival the convenience of academic credit in accountability. But a number of forward-looking faculties in reputable schools are seeking answers. A few promising practices are in trial and prospect. The extended school year is a new device used by schools for providing their own appropriate experiences for in-service growth. Special standing committees elected by the faculty are reviewing proposals by individuals and recommending those of merit to the administration and board for recognition. Other models can be found which hold similar promise.

The profession is seeking more satisfactory answers. Past efforts to apply simple solutions have shown that simple answers won't do. These practices have resulted in the congesting of graduate courses for education specialists with teachers who had little professional need for studies in educational administration, counselling, or psychology. This in turn has resulted in cynicism among some teachers toward the whole area of graduate work in education. Teachers should not be invited or allowed to use their time and resources to accumulate graduate credit in courses not relevant to their teaching. Past excursions of this kind have resulted not only in the cynicism of the teachers but also in the scorn of the public. More alternatives are needed. The requirement that all teachers attend to their own professional development imposes a need to recognize other ways of growing. This would, among other things, benefit graduate study in education.

ON PROFESSIONAL COMPENSATION. To say "a teacher *deserves* appropriate recognition" is to utter an analytic truth. It is a statement no one can contradict. Analytically, the predicate is equivalent to the subject. If the sentence changes to "the teacher *receives* appropriate recognition" it then becomes descriptive of a transaction. It also becomes a massive value problem which turns upon the enormous range of meanings which could be assigned to the words "teacher," "appropriate," and "recognition."

The role of a professional teacher in civilization has been variously commented upon. There is a good deal of romance in it; it has been called colossal. In fact, there is nearly universal agreement that western civilization, as we know it, would shortly dissolve if the functions carried on by professional teachers were either withdrawn or passed along to less able hands. The professional teacher, therefore, is responsible for preserving whatever western civilization claims as its greatness and its gains.

It is also agreed that the teacher has a major role in regard to whatever lies ahead. The future is, as always, clouded by doubt and uncertainty. No one knows exactly what is coming, but we are dazzled at its prospects and appalled by its dangers. There is little certainty except of the knowledge that those who study in our classrooms today will face decisions which are unprecedented in human history.

The professional teacher has the future in his classroom, he prepares the way for it, and he helps develop the men and women who will mold it, knowing that these men and women will have to be better than those which have gone before.

How important are teachers? What recognition does a good teacher deserve? It would be impossible to find a role which exceeds teaching in cruciality. It is difficult to find careers which rival it in importance. But with sublime ease we identify a great array of services which western society rewards more handsomely. This paradox is obviously unrighteous and unwise and reflects unfavorably upon both the morals and the intelligence of western man.

The paradox is strong, but not strange. Western man is not designedly immoral or deliberately unintelligent. In fact, he is inclined to resent suggestions about the inadequacy of either his morals or mind. The contradiction is explained by the history and functions of two western institutions: the free market and the Christian Church. Understanding the problem of teachers' salaries requires among the other things an examination of this context.

In a free market the monetary value of services tends to be regulated by demand and availability. The demand for teaching beyond that provided by the home and the church was, until recent times, quite limited. Qualitative expectations were similarly low, and the numbers of persons available who could meet those expectations were more than adequate. Hence, the operations of the market tended to depress the monetary reward for teaching.

At the peak of Athenian culture a few sophists drew relatively large sums for their teaching. Some of the great teachers were members of the aristocracy. On the other hand, some abstained from a materialistic return and maintained and developed ascetic personal existence. No clear pattern developed prior to the emergence in the seventh century of the Christian Church as the principal teaching institution in western civilization. It was in this era that scholarship and teaching took on some of the monastic features still honored in academic rites. Much teaching was done by clerics who required little payment. This did little to develop a tradition of high monetary

remuneration for the services of teachers. On the contrary, it tended
to remove the work of teaching from among those to be rewarded
by treasures of the earth and aligned it with those to be more amply
recognized in eternity.

Assuredly, modern professional teachers are not prepared to reject
this latter idea. But as education moved out front and beyond the
operations of the religious establishment, and as teaching became
increasingly detached from its ecclesiastical moorings, it became more
clearly a profession *per se*. As such, it is more and more recognized
as a field which one can enter and in which one can seek distinction
as he might also in engineering, law, medicine, or any other area of
essential service. Increasingly, it is a field from which can be expected
such remuneration as the services warrant.

In the present century the body of professional teachers, in
negotiation with the governmental agencies which act in behalf of
the public, began to institute qualitative standards on licensing which
had the effects of improving the caliber of professional teachers and
imposing reasonable limits on the amount of teaching service available. This, against a background of increasing demand, is influencing
a rise in the monetary value of the teaching service. The moral
justification for this exists in the great social benefits which result
from having a corps of highly qualified teachers as opposed to the
conditions existing during the previous century.

This is not, as some may argue, instituting a control over the
market. It is a process whereby society redefines the standards of
teaching appropriate for its needs. An examination of other professions
will find similar processes underway. However, a danger exists in
going too far. If the point is ever reached when professional teachers
institute controls on available service merely for the purpose of
lining the pockets of or providing "rose bed" security for the
current body of practitioners, they then would have arrived at a
position which is morally untenable. Of all the professions, teaching
has the highest obligation to keep its moral foundations intact.

Two burning questions are not discussed here. The first relates
to heavy doubt expressed over the current modes of quality control
in teacher education. The second relates to policies which have
resulted in uniform payment of teachers regardless of effectiveness.
These issues have serious moral components and are of concern in
the matter of appropriate recognition. Let it suffice to say that
teacher education is now a subject of intense inquiry and teachers

themselves are showing increasing interest in programs which contain salary differences based upon evaluated merit. Both these questions are vexing, but if good teachers are to be provided and are to get the recognition they deserve, *both questions must be resolved*.

Finally, it must be recognized that this discourse has focused mainly on the monetary recognition only. In this regard, it is impossible to know with precision what "appropriate recognition" is. However, it is very clear that at present the salaries of good teachers are far less than appropriate. It is equally clear no changes are in immediate prospect which would greatly improve things. Adequate advances can come only if the ideals of quality or excellence in teaching become more satisfactorily defined and identified.

Teachers, however, will not ever become millionaires by teaching alone. If vast wealth is of great importance to a man, he had better choose other work. Money is an important and interesting concern to everyone, but the cardinal reasons a young person becomes a teacher stem from internal commitments he holds toward the intangibles of life and the world which surrounds him. If, after a most thorough examination of these commitments, he finds them in control of his preferences, and if he finds them best fulfilled by the kind of thing professional teachers do, then he should try to become a professional teacher.

He probably will not become wealthy in the conventional sense, but he will be comfortable. The great material luxuries of the world may never be his, but he is quite probably the sort whose existence perceives values others can not perceive. Ultimately, therefore, the question of appropriate recognition vanishes into the personality of the teacher and the satisfactions he derives from the work he does.

As time goes along, this civilization probably will pay its teachers more—a great deal more—, and this is as it should be. But this writer records the hope that money will never become the principal reason men teach. If it does, teaching will not be what it is now and western civilization will commence its own decline and fall. The philosophy of compensation is that important.

NAME INDEX

A

Abelard, 132-134
Achilles, 22
Acumenus, 28
Adam, 27
Agathon, 20, 27-30
Alcibiades, 33-34, 36-37
Anselm, 132
Aphrodite, 21-23
Apollodorus, 20
Aquinas, 51, 94, 123, 146
Aristodemus, 20
Aristophanes, 21, 24-27, 101
Aristotle, 14, 51, 58, 67, 86, 94-95,
    118, 120, 132, 137, 146-149, 161
Augustine, 51, 86, 131, 146
Augustus, Phillip, 134

B

Bach, 93
Becket, 94
Benét, S. V., 92
Bernard, Henry, 154
Boethius, 131
Bridgman, 118
Buber, Martin, 77-78

C

Caesar, Augustus, 94, 131
Caesar, Tiberius, 131
Cajetan, 123
Carson, Rachel, 93
Channing, William E., 85
Charlemagne, 133
Chaucer, 89
Chiron, 131
Christ, 57, 60-61, 72, 90
Coleridge, S., 93
Comenius, 149

D

De Quincy, 151
Descartes, René, 86, 116
Dewey, John, 94, 109, 149, 158
Dickens, Charles, 44
Dionysius, 21
Diotima, 30-33, 36

E

Emerson, Ralph Waldo, 42, 93, 152
Ephesus, 145
Eryximachus, 21, 24-25, 27-28
Euthyphro, 63

F

Fechner, 77-78
Ficino, Marcilio, 21
Freud, Sigmund, 80
Froebel, 149

G

Gershwin, George, 92
Gibbon, Edward, 117
Glaucon, 20
God, 30, 32, 55, 61-62, 73-80, 84, 91,
    93, 96, 116, 146
Grube, G. M. A., 25

H

Hamlet, 150
Harris, William, 154
Hartshorne, Charles, 77
Hector, 22
Hegel, 117, 146
Heidegger, 3, 45
Heine, Heinrich, 55
Heraclitus, 24, 86, 145
Hercules, 131
Hesiod, 21, 31
Homer, 22, 31
Hoover, Herbert, 57

SUBJECT INDEX